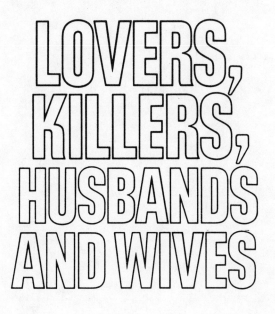

LOVERS, KILLERS, HUSBANDS AND WIVES

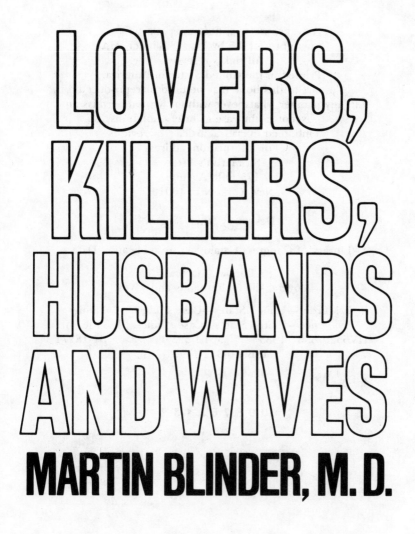

LOVERS, KILLERS, HUSBANDS AND WIVES

MARTIN BLINDER, M. D.

ST. MARTIN'S PRESS □ NEW YORK

Design by Janet Tingey

Library of Congress Cataloging in Publication Data

Blinder, Martin.
Lovers, killers, husbands and wives.

1. Murder—United States—Case studies.   2. Family
violence—United States—Case studies.   I. Title.
HV6529.B56   1985   364.1'523'0973   84-18274
ISBN 0-312-49964-7

10 9 8 7 6 5 4 3 2

FOR
ADAM AND LILAH

ACKNOWLEDGMENTS

There would be no book at all were it not for LFB, Vicki Cederquist, Joyce Cole, Mary Lou Coyle, Herbert Gold, Ruth Potter, Barry Schwenkmeyer, Patricia Shelton, Lisa Wager, and Jayne Walker.

They know it and I know it.

CONTENTS

PREFACE

WHY DO so many people kill for "senseless" reasons, and so very often kill those crucial to them emotionally? What might cause a mother to take the life of her child, or a man that of the woman he deeply loves?

Indeed, most killers and their victims have a pre-existing relationship, usually a close, caring one: In America, the bedroom is second only to the highway as the scene of slaughter. Are there as many different explanations for these perverse acts of devotion as there are homicides? Or is there a common bond amongst amative killers—a shared inability to continue to live in their worlds unless they commit this most unsanctionable of acts?

Like many of us, I had long been mystified by these intimate savageries. The motives typically offered by their perpetrators seemed so inadequate to the deed. Press reports of psychiatric explanations given at time of trial by my colleagues often appeared even less plausible. And the spate of books by journalists, each detailing the life and crime of a particular killer, though providing minute details about the idiosyncratic thoughts and behavior of a single lethal individual, emitted a beam of light too narrow to illuminate the dark, enormous mass that constitutes the psychology of murder.

In time, a need to find my own answers drew me to the

field of forensic psychiatry and to the courts, where I began a personal study of people who kill. The nearly three hundred killers I have subsequently interviewed during the course of two decades of work within the criminal justice system have taught me a great deal about the psychological processes that can lead one human to destroy another—at times almost casually, but more often with the singular intensity characteristic of a compelling love relationship.

To share these insights, in these pages I shall introduce to you ten people within whom love and hate collide catastrophically. Though superficially similar in that they all killed at a time of great passion or despair, each had different underlying motivations; together they provide a fairly complete picture of the unconscious psychodynamics of homicide. I present their stories essentially as told to me, though condensed a bit, grouped together and annotated so as to clarify the psychological and legal issues raised.

Certainly such momentous revelations of feelings and behavior would be absolutely privileged if made by patients to their own psychotherapists. No confidences are breached here, however, for each of these forensic interviews became part of the public record at trial if not before, and their contents in many cases were widely disseminated in the press. Nevertheless, I have chosen to use the individuals' first names only and have altered other potential means of identification for whatever protection such partial anonymity may provide, given the wounds still lingering in their communities. The one exception is that of former San Francisco supervisor Dan White, whose well-publicized crime vitiates any attempts at disguise—there just aren't many men known to have shot and killed the mayor of their city and then also kill a fellow legislator.

These studies are prefaced by a discussion of the function of psychiatric testimony within the American criminal justice system—a topic that has attracted much media attention and some vitriolic criticism during the past few years, in the wake of the White trial and those of John Hinckley and several others. It is not my intention to present a polemical defense of psychiatry, but simply to show how forensic psychiatrists gather clinical evidence, and to familiarize the reader with some of the legal concepts implicit in the narratives that follow. I hope, however, that a cumulative effect of these chapters will be the support of my conviction that psychiatric testimony, even when conflicting, can serve an important function in the courtroom; that defendants who plead insane need—and society is better for having given them—an opportunity to explain what drove them to kill; and that even those who are "successful" in their insanity pleas rarely escape responsibility for their acts.

Finally, the men and women whose voices emerge from these pages together provide a substantive introduction to the psychology of murder, etching coherent clinical patterns upon initially senseless, inchoate violence. Listen to all of them if you can, and seemingly incomprehensible evil will transform itself into meaningful acts, credible diagnoses, and an integral part of the human condition.

"His passion cast a mist before his sense,
And either made, or magnified the offence."

Dryden, *Palamon and Arcite*, Bk ii, 1.334

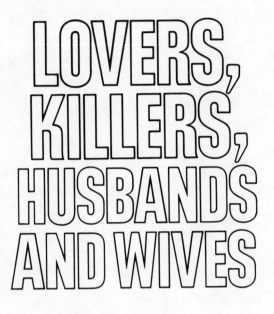

LOVERS, KILLERS, HUSBANDS AND WIVES

INTRODUCTION

THE COURT PSYCHIATRIST AND THE HOMICIDE CASE

I N THE STREET in front of a dozen witnesses, a man fatally shoots two people at random, without provocation. He is apprehended with the still-warm revolver in his hand and is brought to trial. There is no possible doubt of the man's guilt. What purpose could psychiatric testimony serve in his trial? Does it matter that the defendant may be in some way deranged? Admittedly, anyone killing two strangers for no apparent reason has *something* wrong with him, but what of it? *He* alone shot those people . . . nobody else made him do it. With evidence this clear, why should we need more than a simple one-day trial? What could a court psychiatrist do, save to muddle the issues and confuse the jurors?

These questions have long followed forensic psychiatrists from courthouse to courthouse; when verdicts are reached that are socially or politically repugnant (though entirely appropriate from both legal and psychological perspectives), people become angry. But when John Hinckley was found "not guilty by reason of insanity" after having shot President Reagan and two of his aides in full view of the national press corps, public furor brought the controversy concerning the use of psychiatric testimony in criminal trials rolling to a boil.

Critics of these unpopular outcomes, however, most of whom demand that psychiatrists be banished from all criminal trials, possess either a minimal or distorted understanding of just what a forensic psychiatrist does, a situation this book aspires to improve. Certainly they have forgotten that well before a psychiatrist ever entered an American courtroom, our legal system was already greatly concerned not only with *what* a man did wrong, but with *why* he did it—what was going on in his head at the moment of his offense.

It is a cornerstone of our system of justice that if a man perceives himself as innocent at the time of his offense, if he had not *intended* a wrongful outcome, then he is less culpable than someone whose crime was *deliberate* and committed with malice aforethought. Because of the preeminence of the principle that there are *degrees* of criminal liability, criminal trials necessarily go beyond the black-and-white issue of whether or not the accused pulled the trigger, and into the murky labyrinth of his intentions and motivations—his state of mind.

As he fired the gun, did he have his wits about him? Did he know full well, for example, that he was shooting two highway patrolmen? Or was he in the throes of a psychotic delusion, believing, like the schizophrenic man I recently examined, that: "I was warding off these blue devils who had come to steal my soul, and let me tell you, I was only their first victim—if I didn't stop them they'd get every Christian soul"? Did he understand that he was committing an unlawful act or did he think, in his madness, that he was performing a great public service or perhaps even an act of self-defense? In short, though undoubtedly committing the physical act, did he know what he was doing and that it was wrong?

Questions concerning the defendant's state of mind at the time the crime was committed are crucial ones not only in those relatively few* felony trials in which the insanity defense is explicit, but in many other cases. Let me illustrate how strongly such considerations are embedded in our system of criminal justice by use of four different hypothetical scenarios of marital strife (in fact, not all that hypothetical in my forensic practice) during which a husband *physically* brings about the death of his wife. Though in none of them is the husband's sanity necessarily at issue, inevitable variations in verdicts and sentences will depend almost entirely upon the juries having differentiated the *feelings* and *motivations* within each man at the moment of his wife's demise.

Let us first suppose that a man has gradually reached his limits with his abusive, querulous wife of twenty years. One morning, after weeks of thought, he calmly enriches her oatmeal with a lethal pinch of arsenic.

Alternatively, suppose that he joins his wife at breakfast with long-simmering anger but no intention of doing her harm. He promptly gets caught up in another of their terrible marital disputes and finally, in a rage, picks up her oatmeal bowl and smashes it against her skull with deliberately lethal force.

Or, less malignantly, he loses his temper and merely tosses oatmeal in her face, but she falls backward and suffers a fatal skull fracture.

Or, perhaps, he simply shouts at her that he never

* less than 1%

wants to see her again, storms out of the kitchen and into the garage, climbs into their station wagon and, without looking behind him, barrels backward at full speed. Failing to observe his wife chasing after him, still trying to make her point, he runs her over, crushing her skull.

Though none of our four disputatious wives are any the less dead, their respective husbands are not equally guilty, their degree of legal culpability depending in great measure upon what it was they were thinking at the moment of their wives' dispatch. And here there are great differences.

It is hard to imagine a jury finding our wife-poisoner guilty of anything less than premeditated *first degree* murder. But the second husband would likely be found guilty of no more than murder in the *second degree* (because he wished his wife dead only in a brief, furious moment); the third man of *voluntary* manslaughter (in that he wished his wife some slight injury but did not intend her death); and our agitated driver of only *involuntary* manslaughter (because he probably intended his wife no injury whatsoever).

These gradations of culpability reflect time-honored legal principles affirmed every day, in every American criminal court. The insanity defense is no more than a logical extension of these habitual distinctions, all of which depend upon what was going on in the accused's mind at the time of his crime. Indeed, there has been judicial notice that some poor souls have "something missing," and so deserve special consideration, almost as long as there have been laws, and well before the existence of psychiatry (the first case of jury acquittal by reason of insanity was recorded in England in 1505).

The legal definition of insanity most used today dates

back 140 years. In London, on January 20, 1843, Daniel M'Naghten, a drifter with a history of a paranoid mental illness and radical political beliefs, fired a pistol at Prime Minister Robert Peel, whose carriage was just leaving 10 Downing Street. He missed Peel but fatally wounded his companion and private secretary. At M'Naghten's trial, seven psychiatrists (then called alienists) testified that he was mentally deranged, and the jury, after but a few moments' deliberation, agreed: M'Naghten was acquitted by reason of insanity and remanded to a mental institution where he remained until his death twenty-three years later.

The press was outraged, calling the verdict and legal system "absurd," "irresponsible," "crude," "malevolent," and dictated by "seven mad doctors." Even the ordinarily circumspect Queen Victoria complained publicly that "The law may be perfect, but how is it that whenever a case where the application arises, it proves to be of no avail?" and with perplexing syntax expressed incredulity "that anyone could be insane who wanted to murder a conservative Prime Minister."

The House of Lords, however, whose lifelong sinecure afforded them the luxury of judicial dispassion, calmly memorialized England's insanity statutes according to the criteria the court had used to excuse M'Naghten:

> To establish a defense on the grounds of insanity, it must be clearly proved that, at the time of the committing of the act, the party accused was labouring under such a defect of reason, from disease of the mind, as not to know the nature and quality of the act he was doing; or if he did know it, that he did not know he was doing what was wrong.

The M'Naghten Rule served for almost a century and a half as the standard for measuring the mental state of an accused in England and a number of other countries, including the United States. In essence, it relieves the defendant of responsibility for his crime if, because of mental disease or defect, he did not *know the nature, quality, or wrongfulness* of his acts. As the defendant himself might explain, "I didn't know what I was doing."

There have been many modifications of M'Naghten in various jurisdictions during the ensuing 140 years; most liberalize the criteria by which a jury might acquit. For example, the federal courts and some state courts have adopted insanity formulae patterned after the American Law Institute's 1962 model penal code which excuses the defendant when, because of mental illness, he lacks the *capacity either to appreciate the criminality* (or wrongfulness) *of his conduct or to control his actions.* Such a defendant might say, "I couldn't help doing what I did" or "I didn't know that what I did was wrong."

Another version permitted in several states is the "partial insanity" or "diminished capacity" defense, which allows for mitigation of the accused's culpability to the extent that mental illness impairs the *clarity of his thinking* or his *ability to premeditate, harbour malice, or form intent.* In cases of this kind, the defendant might argue, "I didn't really mean to do it."

Just recently, however, a number of states have greatly altered their insanity statutes to favor conviction. For example, in 1982, California voters, in direct response to the Dan White verdict (discussed later in this book), angrily challenged the utility and morality of one of the country's most liberal insanity statutes and passed a citizen's initiative holding that a man might be found insane only if he did not understand the nature *and* quality *and* wrongfulness of his acts. Thus, were he to have the slightest sliver of his wits about him at the moment of his offense, he would be presumed sane. By such criteria it is doubtful whether Daniel M'Naghten himself would have been acquitted, since he fully understood the lethal effect his actions would have upon a man whose identity and onerous political views were well known to him.

Ironically, from Victoria's time to today, even the most vociferous opponent of the *not guilty by reason of insanity* (NGI) statutes would have thought it unfair to hold a severely mentally disabled individual who had committed a crime out of madness to the same legal standard as a normal individual who had rationally, deliberately, and profitably gone about his nefarious business; nor would he likely favor punishing in the usual way a person who simply could not help what he or she did. But when even ostensibly enlightened members of the public witness the logical application of their own reasoning to a particularly unsavory individual who has committed a prominent and heinous crime, they become indignant.

Insanity defenses thus are being stringently limited and even stripped from the books by legislators responding to the anger of their constituents.* Psychiatrists, the obvious clinical vehicle of these unwelcome trial outcomes, have not been recipients of so much animosity since Freud began publicizing the rank eroticism of the unconscious mind. This new and popular public antipathy for forensic psychiatry has even spawned a new

---

* As early as 1973, then President Richard Nixon proposed to Congress the abolition of the insanity defense, thereby denying this last shield to hapless, mentally impaired lawbreakers, none of whom ordinarily would enjoy access to a presidential pardon.

subspecialty of psychiatrist who earns a comfortable living rushing from court to court testifying that psychiatrists have no business testifying in court.

Interestingly, juries who acquit or find reduced culpability are otherwise part of that same exercised public, presumably sharing its fear of the accused, its ignorance of the fact that almost without exception killers of passion kill but once, and its displeasure with easy acquittal. After all, juries tend to be drawn from the most stable, traditional, and conservative members of a community: homeowners, churchgoers, and registered voters. They bring all of their prosecutorial prejudices into the courtroom. Yet, by trial's end, they often put them aside and find the defendant less culpable.

Why? Are they confused by some arcane defense theory? Does a charismatic psychiatrist called by the defendant's attorney hoodwink them?

Hardly.

What happens is that during the course of trial they receive an education. They learn that there is *crime* and then there is *madness.* And they learn that offenders, particularly the violent offenders you will meet later in these pages, are not all the same, nor are their offenses merely the simple, deliberate, and malevolent deeds they appear at first blush to be.

Of course, no one has perfect access to "the truth, the whole truth, and nothing but the truth" concerning a defendant's mind and motives at the moment he commits a crime—not the defendant himself, months or even hours later, and certainly not the forensic psychiatrist, such as myself, who does not get to interview him until sometime before the trial. But, in the absence of divine omniscience, psychiatrists are one of the better instruments thus far discovered by society to give judge and jury access to the mental state of the defendant. We have been trained to listen, sometimes for days on end, to the defendant's history (a life story as well as a narrative of the immediate circumstances of the act), make clinical sense of it, and then translate the ensuing diagnosis into language the layman can understand. In any event, for better or worse, juries faced with the alien task of judging a killer are attentive when I testify, and most judges seem to think that, on my better days at least, I have something to contribute.

During my two decades serving the court, I have most often been asked by the judge to serve as the court's expert, to interview the defendant, report my findings to the bench, and then make myself available during the trial for questioning by both prosecution and defense. Other times, I have been consulted by defense attorneys contemplating the presentation of mitigating psychological evidence they hope will help the jury understand why their clients did what they did. I have also been called by prosecutors who anticipate some sort of psychiatric plea and are particularly interested in any data that might show that, despite impaired thinking or an emotional disorder, the defendant well knew what he was about when he broke the law.

Occasionally I have the opportunity to examine the accused immediately after the homicide, while there is still blood on his or her hands, as it were—though far more often I am not brought into the case until months later and must therefore reconstruct a fading historical event. Frequently I am able to obtain and interpret police reports and past psychiatric records, as well as interview witnesses to the offense and people who may have had opportunity to observe the defendant recently or in the past. Finally, in every case I will have spent many hours preparing to be called to trial, pulling my clinical findings together and rendering them into a form I hope will be comprehensible to people with no psychiatric training.

Quite often that call never comes. The case may be plea bargained to a verdict, or, even if it proceeds to trial, a shift in legal strategy may render psychological factors irrelevant. Or sometimes the attorney who initially requested the consultation may elect not to call me as a witness if, upon marshaling his best case, he finds that my testimony would not support the line of argument he intends to pursue.

The latter circumstance, far from rare, is indicative of the potential conflict between the professional interests of psychiatrists and of lawyers. The forensic psychiatrist must strive to keep himself free of the kind of bias that is the *raison d'être* of the legal advocate. His testimony should be confined to the clinical data so that, in any particular case, it would be much the same, irrespective of who invited his participation.

In practice, of course, many trials in which psychiatric testimony plays a major role have at least two psychiatrists in the courtroom, one on either side, and much has been made of the "battle of the experts" that purportedly ensues. In my experience, however, psychiatrists on opposing sides and even of quite different "schools" will usually describe a defendant's behavior in similar terms ("disoriented"; "tearful") and only slightly less frequently arrive at the same psychiatric diagnosis ("schizophrenia"; "psychotic depression"; "acute drug toxicity"). The diagnostic classifications of the kinds of people who are likely to break down in a criminal way and the nature and mechanisms of the stresses most likely to bring them to this point are, *psychiatrically* speaking, rather well-defined, despite some variations in nomenclature. Usually, it is only when psychiatrists are asked to leave the clinical field and comment on such conundrums as "premeditation," "intent," or "malice" —all legal rather than psychological concepts—that vast differences in interpretation can and often do emerge.

In short, far from the din of adversarial procedures, psychiatrists have little trouble agreeing among themselves whether or not a man is mentally ill. But a psychiatric diagnosis of *psychosis* is not a synonym for the more narrowly defined legal concept of *insanity*. Most mentally ill people are as capable of distinguishing right from wrong as the rest of us. Even a man with a long history of schizophrenia can rationally, if unlawfully, decide that an easier living may be made holding up liquor stores than washing dishes. Operating in these instances out of the nonpsychotic part of his mind, he could hardly expect to be found insane: Fulminating schizophrenia itself guarantees no immunity to larceny. The extreme sociopath, who is constitutionally unable to conform his behavior to social norms, is excluded entirely from most current legal formulae for diminished liability because he *knows,* cognitively speaking, when he is breaking the law; though doubtless mentally ill from a clinical perspective, legally he is fully responsible for his antisocial actions.

What really matters then in the courtroom is not so much the diagnosis of a mental disorder as is its severity and pervasiveness: its effect on a man's ability to function within a particular social context. Here, even conflicting psychiatric testimony will help the jury to comprehend the emotional makeup of the defendant and the circumstances leading him to crime. Implicitly, such testimony may also provide the jury with an instrument for expressing a degree of identification with, or disaffection for, the accused. If a juror can *understand* how it could happen that someone like himself—very much a peer—could kill, he will use defense psychiatric testimony as a device for finding the defendant less culpable. If, on the other hand, everything he has seen and heard in the courtroom leaves him feeling repelled by the defendant and fearful of him, he will employ prosecution psychiatric testimony to minimize the legal relevance of the man's mental disorder, however deranged he appears to be.

But this is, finally, how the American legal system is *supposed* to work—a trial, not by experts, but by the defendant's peers. Once adequately informed, the jury is surely better able than the psychiatrist to determine the significance and relevance of a defendant's disorder in his particular milieu. And so the doctor, having offered his clinical picture of the accused, should put down his brush, quit the courtroom, and leave the jury to contemplate and give name to the painting: to draw its own legal conclusions in the light of prevailing levels of understanding, insight, compassion, and anger in the community. It is my hope that you will engage yourself in just such a process as you go forward in this book.

The portraits that you are about to examine of individuals who have killed have a higher degree of immediacy than I am able to present in a courtroom. In my forensic reports or at trial I describe and analyse such people who themselves rarely testify. In these pages, however, they talk to you largely in their own words.

Though what they say is perhaps not the "whole truth," it is as close as we are likely to come to their own individual truths about homicide.

They will demonstrate the traps men and women can build for themselves from which there is none but a lethal escape, or reveal delusional worlds wherein an utterly irrational act makes perfect sense. They will describe ineluctable feelings of impotency, dependency, and helplessness. They will illuminate the singularly ruthless efficiency of minds unfettered by conscience. Together, they can tell you why people kill.

Let me now withdraw and allow them to speak for themselves.

THE
DISSOCIATIVE
KILLER

During the course of our lives, each of us is bound to encounter situations exceeding our coping ability, and bringing us great conflict, anxiety, and emotional pain. Such is the price of being human. When that price becomes intolerably high, however, some uniquely vulnerable individuals may be triggered into a dissociative state: an essentially unconscious, psychological splitting mechanism that defends against emotional distress and softens the impact of the threatening situation.

During this dissociative episode we see a segregation and isolation of otherwise closely related parts of the personality; usually well-integrated patterns of perception, thought, feeling, and behavior become sequestered from conscious control and awareness. An ordinarily rational person fails to recognize the obvious, and acts in a fashion totally at odds with his characteristic behavior and fundamental beliefs. The amnesic splits off unwanted memories. The multiple personality splits off entire unacceptable parts of himself.

An analogous process, and one very common in medicine, is that of the denial of death by a clearly terminal cancer patient who has slipped closer to the end after each of three palliative operations, but continues to ignore his weakness, pain, and dramatic weight loss, the pessimism of his physicians, the distress of loved ones. Instead, he cheerfully plans for next year's vacation, studiously avoids preparing a will, and makes long-range business commitments that fail to allow for the great probability of his not being there to execute them.

Psychological defense mechanisms, though they allay anxiety, do not eliminate its causes. They reduce neither underlying conflicts nor their power to produce aberrant thoughts or behavior. In short, dissociation, like other defense mechanisms, though often "successful," can create problems in its own right: The cancer patient may face death with ignorant equanimity but leave his estate in costly disarray.

As the next two chapters demonstrate, an acute and potentially lethal dissociation may occur when someone discovers that his survival depends upon reconciling the irreconcilable. Overwhelmed, his mind leaves the scene, taking with it judgment and restraint. Primordial instincts can then direct behavior, briefly free *of any awareness of the need to conform to social mores or obey the law.*

THE PERFECT COUPLE

ONLY LOVE for his wife, Roslyn, exceeded Solly's love of gambling. He gambled so enthusiastically, so dauntlessly—on indolent horses, desultory football teams, on almost any object that moved (however slowly)—that at the time of Roslyn's death Solly owed bookmakers over one hundred thousand dollars.

There was more. Because Roslyn condemned his gambling losses but happily appropriated his occasional winnings as routinely as she did his salary check, Solly frequently took to telling her that he had won, proving it with money borrowed from the bank for just this purpose.

"You see," Solly explained, "handling money always cheered Roslyn up—always." Therefore, as he assured me several times during my examination of him in the Albuquerque jail, the love he felt for her justified the debt of nearly another hundred thousand dollars to various banks, on top of that due the bookmakers.

Then Roslyn's brother, Morris, fired him. The ensuing added financial pressures triggered the first episodes since childhood of Solly's sleepwalking, and these in turn led to his brutally taking the life of the woman he so cherished.

The week that I performed my psychiatric evaluation—on behalf of the defense—Solly's trial was only days away. He faced certain conviction for murder unless a jury could make sense of what he had done or perhaps discover some means, if not to excuse or forgive, at least to understand sufficiently to find him less culpable. Yet, four months since his wife's death, Solly himself was still psychologically unable to accept his having taken her life.

He leaned forward as he spoke—softly, earnestly, persuasively. "She was the most important person in the world, Doctor. She did everything perfectly—the way she created and cared for our home, for our daughters, the way she dressed. Doctor, Roslyn was perfect in every way. I know I did what I did, but I don't believe it. It makes no sense."

"Some people might find living with all that perfection something of a burden," I observed. Solly just looked at me blankly, so I turned our attention to the less-threatening subject of his past. "Shortly, I would like you to tell me a great deal more about Roslyn and your relationship with her. But let me get a little background first."

Solly told me about his childhood in Chicago during the 1950s, his being thrust out on his own at a fairly early age by his father's premature death, his workaholic success in several business ventures, his marriage fifteen years before to Roslyn when both were in their early twenties, and their move six years earlier to Albuquerque, where he ended up working as operations manager of his brother-in-law's restaurant business. Solly saw himself as having become an extraordinarily contented, well-adjusted person who thoroughly enjoyed his happy marriage, the affection of his two young daughters, a good job and income, and the comforts of a well-appointed home. He and Roslyn were known to most of their friends and to their larger social community as "the perfect couple." Indeed, during our first meeting, Solly would admit to only two tiny, dark clouds floating high above his luminous life: a history (shared with a sister) of sleepwalking as a child, and his compulsive gambling. Yet, I was to discover that his gambling, though certainly productive of enormous losses and financial pressure, as a cause of emotional stress, paled beside his relationship with Roslyn.

It wasn't until well into our second session that Solly permitted this to begin to surface. But once he allowed me to tug on the first loose thread of a marital problem, two more threads came free, followed by four, and by interview's end, the entire fabric of his "perfect" marriage had unraveled.

To begin with, Roslyn managed their financial affairs with formidable competence; because she spent money so wisely, she got to spend it all. Their income, he insisted, reflected a model division of labor—he earned it, she spent it. He would turn his weekly check over to her, and each morning she would dole back a little cash for that day's expenses. She had seven credit cards, he had none.

"It worked, Doctor, because Roslyn knew how to use money. It was because of *Roslyn,* you know, that we had this enormous show-place home. She knew how to buy clothes . . . I never saw her look less than smashing. And though she always bought the best, she always had something left to put away in her savings."

"*Her* savings?"

"Oh yes, they were hers—since *she* was able to save it, it was *her* money. We were never going to touch that."

"Where'd you get the money to gamble?"

"My commissions came in cash. Roslyn didn't know that."

"Let me ask—what kind of car did you drive?"

"A Toyota."

"And Roslyn?"

"A Seville."

"I am satisfied that Roslyn was a brilliant homemaker, but it still seems remarkable that you could afford all of this, plus the gambling, on—what were you making? About forty thousand dollars a year?"

"Well, we got the house for nothing down—a really good deal. Then we refinanced twice. And we bought a lot on credit. It made a lot of sense then with inflation the way it was."

"How many hours a day would you work to maintain all this good sense?"

"It varied. Usually ten, maybe twelve."

"And weekends?"

"I worked a lot of weekends too."

"I guess Roslyn was pretty proud to have a man willing to put so much of himself into making sure she had what she wanted."

Solly didn't reply. I let the silence build until he felt he had to say something.

"Well, actually, that wasn't Roslyn's way . . ."

"Her way?"

"I mean—she wasn't one to hand out bouquets."

As it turned out, it wasn't Roslyn's way to say "thank you" either. As Solly began to look with less denial at his transactions with Roslyn, he was gradually able to perceive and acknowledge that much of what he did was taken for granted, while failures never went unnoticed. Roslyn kept him informed up to the minute about the discrepancy between the prices of things they needed and the size of his paycheck. She was quick to note and comment upon the apparent modesty of his commissions, the infrequency of his raises. But she was oblivious to the growing size of their debts and continued to spend at a fixed rate for "what we just have to have."

She seemed equally disinterested in his opinions and tastes. He might come home one day and find an entirely new bedroom set installed. Never a discussion as to his color preference or whether he felt they needed or could afford it—she just went out and bought it. A perfect purchase.

But this is not to say that Roslyn acted impetuously and without advice, for she consulted almost daily with her mother over lunch and spoke with her no less than two hours a day by phone. "She was a devoted daughter," said Solly. "She and her mother shared everything. Before Roslyn made a move, she talked it over with her mother. She's a very powerful woman. She's already got custody of my kids."

The financial denouement occurred during the last six months of Roslyn's life, when she refused to modify her spending relative to her husband's loss of job and income, adding measurably to their debts, and providing fuel for now open, strident arguments. For both of them, addiction to the procurement and spending of money overlay an exceeding sense of deprivation and loss. Remorselessly, Roslyn pressured Solly to find more money while her buying continued without relationship to their ability to pay. Shortly before her death, Roslyn had been out road-testing a new Cadillac; the following day she and her mother had gone searching for a larger house in a "more established neighborhood." In turn, to cover his earlier debts and produce further apparent winnings to ameliorate the escalating conflict with Roslyn, Solly gambled and borrowed, gambled and borrowed.

At this juncture, the perfect couple was quarreling from the moment Solly entered the house each evening. Solly described how Roslyn would harangue him for hours, until either she would run down or he would leave the room exhausted and exasperated, and then the next day—or a week or a month later—she would raise exactly the same issue. Their fights settled nothing. And more likely than not, he'd get a phone call that evening from his mother-in-law, who would pick up where her daughter had left off.

Battles about money entirely supplanted sexual passion, aided by the discovery earlier that year during a routine Pap smear of precancerous cells on Roslyn's cervix. Though these were cauterized completely and without incident, Roslyn, resonating with her mother's gratuitous biomedical research into the relationship between sexual frequency and cervical cancer, began to seek and invariably found reason to avoid sexual intercourse. Frequently she made phone calls to her mother around their eleven P.M. bedtime. By the time mother and daughter were done talking, Solly's sexual moment invariably had passed.

"What events could possibly have occurred between

Roslyn's luncheon conversations with her mother and the evening call that would keep her on the phone for over an hour?"

"I don't know. They always seemed to have lots to gossip about."

"And afterwards?"

"Afterwards we would go to sleep."

"No sex? No conversation?"

"No. Usually not. Except that I would always say 'Good night, Roslyn, I love you.'"

"You *always* did this?"

"Every night, for fifteen years."

"And Roslyn would say . . ."

"Usually Roslyn wouldn't say anything. I would kiss her on the cheek and tell her I loved her. And we would go to sleep."

"Are you saying that you received no loving words, no affection or sex from Roslyn?"

"Well, Roslyn was not affectionate . . . in the usual sense. No kissing or fondling or anything of that sort. She just didn't seem to want . . . want to get involved. But she always gave me head once a week. No matter how Roslyn was feeling, she always took care of me."

"I suppose she did that perfectly too?"

"Roslyn could get me off in two minutes."

As Solly's unproductive search for any kind of work that might pay something approaching his previous salary lengthened from weeks into months, Roslyn focused on him with increasing intensity, demanding that he account for how he spent the day:

"What happened at the job interview? My mother told you never to say anything about that incident

. . . Did you try that other place? Did you speak to my cousin's friend like I told you? What about the guy who called you yesterday? You were supposed to call him back!"

Yet Solly plugged along, seemingly oblivious to his emerging marital disaster and lethal shift in feelings for his wife. His only conscious difficulty in the weeks prior to Roslyn's death was the pounding headache he developed almost every evening within moments of entering the house. But this symptom too was simply grist for Roslyn's inquisitorial mill:

"What is with you—are you sick again? Where are you going—I'm trying to have a conversation with you. Why are you going into the bathroom? What are those pills? You're not supposed to take so much Tylenol—they're bad for your kidneys. Why do you keep having these headaches?"

"Solly—at some level you must have sensed that you and your marriage were in serious trouble . . . that your relationship with Roslyn was—well, to put it straight out —terrible. And getting worse."

"Doctor, at the time I didn't think it was terrible. Perhaps it changed so gradually; I don't know. I didn't see it as bad at all. I was used to Roslyn being somewhat hypersensitive, getting upset when thing—when things . . ."

". . . when things didn't go perfectly." By now *I* needed a little respite from the relentless pain of this relationship, even if Solly thought he didn't. "During the last year, there must have been some good times too, don't you think?"

"Yes . . . yes. We had plenty of good times—we always had good times. We played a lot of tennis, went out to dinner three times a week, went to the club. And Roslyn gave spectacular dinner parties."

"So at least you got to spend some time with people you enjoyed."

No, he didn't. Roslyn didn't care for his friends. She entertained people she "looked up to." Her social prejudices embraced even his family, whom she perceived as decidedly "low-brow." They were invited over only for the occasional, obligatory holiday dinner. Going along with this, Solly became isolated and increasingly confined to his relationship with Roslyn. She was never far from his thoughts or he from hers. The day before she died, she managed to track him down at his last job interview and demanded a report over the phone:

"Roslyn, I'm talking to them now. Can I call you back? I know, Roslyn . . . yes, I will . . . Roslyn, let me call you . . . yes . . . yes . . . look, I will call you back . . ."

I attempted to probe and make explicit the feelings Solly so assiduously denied: "As all this was going on, Solly, how did you feel? Did you ever get angry? Depressed? Didn't you ever want to hit her in the mouth?"

Solly maintained that he felt fine. He never got angry, certainly never struck her—or anyone else in his life. But he acknowledged moments when he could not wait to leave the room.

"I'd just have to get out of there. It felt like my entire body wanted to explode. But I wouldn't do anything. Maybe slam a door. Once I think I hit a wall. But that's all I did. I mean, I love—I loved her . . ."

Astonishingly, throughout this period Solly exhibited no insomnia or loss of appetite, no alcohol or drug abuse. His life presented a resolutely smooth, glassy surface, save for the progressive headaches and the gambling. Then, in May, he started sleepwalking again, just as he had in childhood. Little walks, down the hall, once out to the back patio. Perhaps three or four times, no more.

"Solly, throughout this entire time, you never once considered a divorce?"

"Out of the question. I could never have such an idea! It would mean losing all that I had—my family, my house, my position, my car. And I thought that I never felt anything but love for Roslyn. I certainly don't remember feeling any hatred, I don't remember even getting mad for very long. But I guess I must have, if I did what I did . . ."

At about midnight, on May 27, the night before their fifteenth anniversary, Roslyn was stabbed to death in her bed.

Earlier that evening, Roslyn, Solly, and their two girls had eaten hamburgers for dinner. Solly drank no alcohol, consumed no drugs. At nine-thirty, Solly's brother Larry called about the five thousand dollars they owed him for some years, and then Roslyn followed with a diatribe about how "money-grubbing" Larry and the rest of Solly's family were. From ten-thirty until about eleven-thirty, Roslyn spoke with her mother, repeating her criticism of Larry. Then she climbed into bed alongside him and reminded him "for the tenth time that day to bring home the car by three P.M. tomorrow." As she turned out the light, Solly said good night to Roslyn as he had every night throughout their fifteen-year marriage: "Good night, Roslyn, I love you." He kissed her on the cheek.

She responded in her usual way: She said nothing.

Solly believes he went to sleep. He has no recollection of getting out of bed, walking to the kitchen for the knife, crossing to his wife's side of the bed.

"All I remember is waking up and seeing these two guys in our room. It was like a dream, but I recall that one had a beard, and the room was a mess."

Solly's next recollection is that of seeing one of the intruders by Roslyn's side of the bed, his hand holding a knife poised above her. He watched transfixed by horror and fear as the knife plunged into Roslyn's chest and abdomen fifteen times, once for each year of their marriage. Then the men fled, leaving the bedroom in disarray, dresser drawers torn out and their contents tumbled on the floor, pictures askew, clothes wrenched from hangers and dumped in muddled heaps.

It wasn't until three days later that Solly, lying on a cot in his jail cell, jerked upright with the vivid realization that there had been no intruders. The hand he saw bearing the knife was his own.

The courtroom in which Solly's long trial took place was packed each day with smartly dressed women of about Roslyn's age. Press coverage was extensive and generally quite hostile to the defendant. The jury of six men and six women listened, first to the prosecutor's case: that Solly had staged a phony burglary to cover his deliberate murder of his wife. Then they heard Solly's reappraisal from the witness stand of his idyllic marriage. They heard from a series of neighbors, friends, and relatives who knew the surface of his marriage and had glimpsed the reality beneath. Finally, they heard psychiatric testimony that explained dissociation and sleepwalking and put both in the context of Solly's personal and marital history. Then, after only an hour, the jury returned to the palpitating courtroom—with an acquittal.

Because Solly's moment of insanity and the stress that had produced it had long since passed, he was immediately free of the court's custody. At last report he is living alone and working in Chicago.

FROZEN OUT

DAN WHITE—ex-cop, ex-fireman, and soon-to-be ex-politician—had had enough.

A young political neophyte just elected to San Francisco's byzantine Board of Supervisors, a law-and-order conservative in a hotbed of liberals, he found himself consistently outvoted—or rather, outmaneuvered before issues ever came to a vote. Gone was his image of himself as the honest, effective, fair-haired neighborhood politician for the stolid, middle-class, home-owning, sexually orthodox San Franciscan. Instead, he perceived his nascent career as community leader in tatters due to special-interest pressure, an increasingly hostile press, and the city attorney's decision that forced him to give up his firefighter's job—and income—because of its purported conflict with the financial interest of his position on San Francisco's governing board.

On Monday, November 10, he announced his resignation. The mayor accepted it with apparent reluctance.

Dan's initial sense of relief was followed almost immediately by guilt, a feeling that he had quit a fight—had abandoned his ideals and his supporters. So four days later he told the mayor that he had changed his mind and the mayor said, "Okay, Dan, I think you can be reappointed. Just get up a little public show of support."

Dan soon had the letters and phone calls pouring into City Hall. But to no effect. Mayors too have a right to change their mind.

At nine P.M. on Thursday, November 16, CBS reporter Barbara Taylor phoned Dan and asked for his comment on the mayor's announcement that Dan White would not be reappointed to his seat. Manifestly stunned, he put down the phone without comment. The next morning he showered and dressed, gathered up his .38 caliber service revolver and a handful of shells and went to confront the mayor.

Arriving at City Hall, he circumvented the metal detector by going in through a ground-floor window which served as an *ad hoc* door for City Hall cognoscenti. A few minutes later, he kept Mayor Moscone's last appointment.

He spoke with the mayor for several minutes, then drew his revolver and emptied it at him, firing the last shell at the mayor's head from a distance of a few inches. Mayor Moscone died instantly, a cigarette still burning in his hand.

Dan turned, left the mayor's office, and sped down the hall toward the office of his principal political antagonist, fellow supervisor Harvey Milk.

"I want to talk to you a minute, Harv," Dan said. A few moments later, he emptied his gun again into Supervisor Milk's body and head. He fled, but within the hour, gave himself up to his close friend, Police Inspector Frank Falzone.

Although Dan was charged with premeditated murder, twelve of his peers convicted him only of manslaughter, a verdict carrying a maximum sentence of seven years.

The day after the jury reached its verdict, a large and primarily gay segment of the San Francisco community rioted over what they saw as a gross miscarriage of justice. Shortly thereafter, the electorate, goaded by derision in the press (which was now characterizing defense psychiatric testimony as "the Twinkie defense," a reference to White's penchant for junk food), replaced one of this country's most liberal and sophisticated tests of insanity with the most simplistic and restrictive.

Did justice indeed miscarry? Had you been on the Dan White jury, in court day after day, able to hear and weigh all of the evidence, what verdict would you have reached? Was Dan White's crime the act of a shambles of a man who for several minutes simply did not have his wits about him, or that of a vengeful, calculating killer?

On April 17, 18, and 21 of 1979, five months following the homicides, I examined Dan White on behalf of his attorney. (That same week I was also able to interview his wife, Tina, his sister Nancy, and his aide, Marjorie.) A quiet, square-jawed, muscular, clean-cut, athletic-looking man who projected an "All-American" wholesomeness, Dan was polite, bland, and impassive throughout my nine hours with him. Much of that time, I felt as if I were interviewing a piece of granite. Unblinking, vivid green eyes seemed out of place in his implacably still, neutral countenance. Either an extraordinarily polished liar or uncommonly straightforward, he answered all of my questions without hesitation or apparent guile or evasion.

At the time of my examination, Dan was thirty-two years old. He was the second oldest of four boys and five girls born to Irish-Catholic parents, and like his eight siblings, had spent most of his life in San Francisco.

During our first interview, devoted primarily to our getting a feel for each other and to my obtaining some background about his early years, Dan told me that as a child he felt fairly close to his father—a city fireman—who was by far the more outwardly loving and demonstrative of his parents, but of whose fathering he had felt deprived by the fireman's long hours away from home. Even what paternal attention was available was of necessity spread amongst Dan's eight siblings. When Dan was seventeen, his father died of cancer. Dan felt an uncommon loss, "like I never had a chance to really get to know him, and now I never would."

He described his mother as unruffled, "solid, like a rock. She raised all of her children right, but I always felt that she did so out of a sense of duty—following her head rather than her heart."

Dan does not remember himself as a particularly happy child. No matter what he did, it seems his family criticized him, sometimes subtly, other times more directly.

"I always felt like the black sheep of the family. Misunderstood. Usually the odd man out. They were always putting me down. Always disappointed in me. I guess I grew up feeling different from the very people I most wanted to be accepted by. Finally I kinda gave up on them and pretty much kept my thoughts and feelings to myself."

Indeed, the only family member with whom he ever felt real and enduring kinship was his sister Nancy, six years his junior. With the others he always felt he had to prove himself—and rarely succeeded.

"Did you yourself make no contribution to the difficulties you were having?"

Dan allowed that he was something of a "know-it-all," possessing a bad temper he learned neither to control nor to conceal until his late teens. In public school he got into many fights, but in his view it was never as instigator, but as *rescuer,* someone who stood up for others who were getting pushed around.

"There was this kid, Frank Walker," he explained, matter-of-factly. "I remember his name to this day, a fat kid with glasses who was always being picked on by the class bully. I told this guy that if he wanted a fight, why not take on someone who could give him a good one? We met outside the school and I let him have it."

Dan offered other examples of where, sometimes recklessly, he would stand up for what he believed to be right, using his fists whenever necessary. Understandably, his parents and teachers did not always approve of his pugilistic approach to diplomacy and justice; thus, he remained an outsider.

"I always knew that my sister Nancy cared. She was the only one of my family who never found fault with me. The rest of them . . . Y' know, I can't remember my older brother ever asking me to pal along with him. Not even once. When I was a kid I looked up to him. I missed his support. It bothered me that he always let me down. Funny thing, he was even more of a troublemaker than I was. Only *he* got away with it while I always got caught and punished. I just didn't have his knack." Although I could not know it at that moment, Dan's feelings about his brother were of great importance to understanding his murderous acts.

Dan and his siblings were brought up strict Catholics.

As a youngster, he took parochial instruction literally, attempting to follow it rigidly, "like it was gospel—which I guess it was." His early attempts to live up to what he was taught were followed by later realization that such instruction was "patently ridiculous—just ridiculous to say that it was immoral to eat meat on Friday or to masturbate." By late adolescence he had become quite disillusioned with all aspects of Catholicism and only rarely attended church.

Dan finished high school with an overall B-plus average, and then joined the Army, serving as a paratrooper in Vietnam.

"I'd never seen anything like that before—all of those Vietnamese bodies stacked along the side of the road. It also bothered me that Americans seemed to be hated by the very people we were there to protect. I began to wonder about the point of it all." His Vietnam experience left him questioning the credibility of government authority much as he had questioned church directives several years before.

Shortly after his discharge from the Army, he joined the San Francisco Police Department. Assigned at first as an undercover narcotics agent, he found it quite difficult to—as he put it—"ingratiate" himself with people whom he was ultimately bound to arrest, and so he requested transfer to street patrol.

"Why did you want to be a cop in the first place?"

"I thought that here was a chance to really serve my community."

"That's probably the best reason to be a policeman. Why'd you quit?"

"Because my supervisors in the department did not support or respect their own men. Even the very citizens who we were helping and protecting—they didn't appreciate what we were doing either."

"And when you feel unappreciated . . ."

". . . sooner or later I leave."

Dan had managed to save a good sum of money and decided to take a year off to explore life and some of the world. An avid reader, he had always enjoyed the works of and identified with Jack London, and so consciously chose to follow in his footsteps, heading north to Alaska.

Then, in October of 1971, his money spent, he returned to the police department, although dissatisfaction with the context in which he had to work (as opposed to the work itself) remained. After only fifteen months, he abruptly quit again.

"What happened?"

"I was frozen out. I had broken the code of police brotherhood and silence. One night I found several officers beating up a handcuffed prisoner. I stopped them. Then I pressed charges. That made it really tough for me. Most of the other officers cut me cold. My own lieutenant told me that he would protect a cop up to and including murder. But I did what I felt I had to do. Right is right and wrong is wrong. Period. There was no point in my staying there after that. So I resigned and went back to Alaska."

"It sounds like you really were a man apart—whether it involved your family, the church, the Army, the police department—how about the fire department?"

"The fire department was different."

In January of 1974 he became a firefighter. "I really liked the work—the public service aspects of it—as much as I liked being a policeman. And firemen get a lot more administrative and citizen support."

As a fireman, Dan again found opportunity to express his devotion to the underdog and his unremitting sense of righteousness—going to bat for four rookie firemen who, in his view, were being washed out of the system without just cause. "I got them reinstated in the program. I think because of what I did, the system by which men could become firemen was made more open and fair."

He continued to work as a fireman until his election to the Board of Supervisors.

"Obviously, Dan, I'm going to need a lot of information from you about your experience on the Board. But a bit more background first. Let's move to your personal life, now, if you would. I know that you're a married man . . ."

"Yes, I married in 1976."

"In a word, how has that worked out?"

"Tina has been everything I could ask in a wife . . ." He paused.

"Yes?"

". . . except . . . I haven't always been sure that I *wanted* a wife—not really sure I wanted to take on all those responsibilities. Of course, my family expected that I would do that sort of thing—marry and have children. So I did it. Tina was a schoolteacher. I knew her about eight months. I was thirty when I married her, she was thirty-four. If I ever was going to get married, she would be the one. It was time for me to marry. I felt comfortable with her. So we got married."

"You have a child?"

"Yeah, my son was born a year later."

"I hear clearly that you love your wife, but I also hear

a lot of ambivalence. Before your marriage, you were very social? Did you do much dating and so on?"

"Some. I've always been kind of—cautious—around women. Y' know, you can get very strong feelings . . . I don't think I ever really got over my first big romance when I was sixteen. Since that time I've kind of held my feelings in check."

"But your marriage now is a good one?"

"Yes, it's a good one. Tina is always supportive of whatever I decide. I can't say she is really a confidante— I've never really had a confidante—but whatever I decide is okay with her. I don't know—maybe I might have been happier without the obligations and responsibilities of a wife and family. But it's all worked out."

"Your son is well?"

"Yes."

"He was born . . ."

"July 14, 1978."

"That's just a few months before the shootings, is it not? Were there any difficulties with your son's birth?"

"Not exactly. But I named him after my father. And you know, everyone in my family—except Nancy—criticized me. They said it was 'presumptuous.' I couldn't believe it, but then again, it was just like them."

"Have there been any other women recently figuring in your life?"

"No. Well, there's Marjorie—my aide. She's been invaluable. I really appreciate her. Can't say we're close in a personal sense."

"And men?"

"I guess I haven't ever been close to anyone. I think I'm cordial, but I've always been a loner. I allow my friendships to go only so far. It's always worked out best for me to take care of my own problems. Keep my own counsel. All my life I've been able to handle any problems by myself. If the going got tough, I'd just dig in the harder."

He grimaced. "I guess this time it didn't work. The harder I dug in, the deeper I got. I've had plenty of stress before—as a police officer and paratrooper—but it never fazed me. This time, though, certain things . . ."

"What things?"

"This . . . political thing."

"Politics played an important part in what happened?"

"Yes."

"Tell me about it—how you got into it, what happened to you because of it, anything else you think important."

"Well, you know, the funny thing is, I never was what you would call 'political.' Politicians all seemed pretty much the same to me. Irrelevant. In it for themselves. They had nothing to do with me or the things that mattered to me. But then I started to find out how badly the city was run—the quality of the school system, public safety . . . you know, there is no way the police can protect the citizen if someone is out to hurt him. They may be able to catch the perpetrator later, but that doesn't do his victim very much good. You have to change how things are done *before* crime takes place. You have to change things from the top. I knew that most of the people out there in the neighborhoods agreed with me. I believed that *I* could do something—I could really make some changes. Why write an angry letter to City Hall? Why not *become* City Hall and let people write angry letters to me?"

He calculated that with supervisorial elections now by

district—as opposed to the previous city-wide electoral system—five thousand votes would put him in office, wherein he would have the power to put things right. He thought about it for several weeks and then in July announced his decision to his wife and to the public.

In characteristic manner, he threw everything he had into the campaign, spending all of his savings, going into debt, and relying heavily on newly created personal contacts as compensation for his lack of a political base. He walked every street in his district, visited seven thousand homes, three thousand businesses. When the votes were counted he had confounded the experts—all of whom had rated him a long shot—by winning with a substantial margin. Much of the joy of victory, however, was taken from him by the City Attorney's ruling that he would have to give up his job with the fire department because of a "potential conflict of interest."

"Can you believe that! Here are all these other supervisors who own businesses that deal with the city all the time and no one bats an eye. I promised to abstain on any votes involving the fire department but no dice. The City Attorney insisted that I either give up my job in the fire department or give up my seat on the board."

"Why didn't you fight it?"

"I didn't want to hear any crap that I was greedy, that I wanted two salaries. So I quit my job as a fireman."

Thus, Dan's winning public office in effect cost him ten thousand dollars a year—the difference between his previous salary as fireman and his new salary as supervisor. At the same time, his wife, now in her third trimester of pregnancy, had to leave her teaching job as well, and with it went her sixteen-thousand-dollar annual salary. As a consequence, the Whites suddenly had to get by with a total family income of only twelve thousand dollars a year.

"But what really hurt the most were all those press reports that I was flush with unreported corporate donations—that I was being financed by special-interest fat cats. They were all supposed to be taking good care of me. Well, *no* one was taking care of me. I had had to find a different way of making a living, so I took out a twenty-thousand-dollar second mortgage and opened The Hot Potato [a fast-food restaurant] down on Fisherman's Wharf. Whenever I wasn't involved on the board, I was down there running the shop. And when I wasn't running the shop, Tina was."

"Doesn't sound like the two of you saw much of each other."

"We didn't have much contact at all. Even when we would be home together, we usually would be much too tired to make any use of it."

"Do you think you made the right decision—leaving the fire department in favor of the Board of Supervisors?"

"No—if I had to do it all over again, I would have quit the board and stayed a fireman . . . Well, as you know—eventually I *did* quit the board . . ."

"How did that come about?"

"In the first place, I was blown away by the rampant graft and corruption in City Hall. With the exception of Diane Feinstein and Harvey Milk, you could have bought any of them. I would put in hours wrestling with an issue, trying to find out what was good and what was bad about it. It didn't matter. Nobody votes these things on their merits—it was all politics. They made no bones about it. Someone would tell me, 'This proposal is ridiculous but

I have to go with it—these people own me.' Everything was decided on a personal basis. One supervisor had been given bad seats at a baseball game so he votes against a ball-field tax exemption."

"As they say, I only know what I read in the newspapers, Dan, and the newspapers always wrote of your being the captive of the conservative, big-moneyed, downtown interests. And because of this, you clashed with a lot of other supervisors, particularly Harvey Milk."

"Not so. I think that Harvey and I were the only ones who cared about the individual citizen, the underdog. Most of the others were there to help themselves. It's a matter of record that I went to bat for Harvey, who was on the outs for a time when he failed to support Diane Feinstein for head of the board."

"What did you think about the fact that he was gay?"

"It had nothing to do with me. I may have disagreed with Harvey on a lot of things, but his being gay kinda made him an underdog too. He was willing to stand up for what he believed. He was a natural leader." (Indeed, Tina White reported to me that her husband had on several occasions described Harvey Milk as "hard-working—he has the city at heart." He had spoken also of Mayor Moscone as an "okay guy.")

"But I was treated different from Harvey. Harvey always won his share of votes, I always lost. I felt useless, frustrated, and isolated on that board. Anyway, I couldn't afford being there anymore."

Worse even than being repeatedly outvoted for what he perceived as venal reasons was his portrayal in the press as being anti-black and anti-gay.

"Those were just smears. Look at my voting record. I was for civil rights as much as anyone."

"But then, you did vote against the Gay Rights Ordinance . . ."

". . . because I don't believe any one group should be singled out for special considerations. That's not civil rights, that's civil privilege."

"Was there any kind of coalition—any allies you had during these struggles?"

"No. I always kept my own counsel before, I handled things myself then, too. Until I couldn't handle it any more."

"Then . . ."

"Then I quit."

"Was this a sudden—an impulsive decision to resign your seat? What were you feeling at the time you decided you wanted out?"

It was at this point that Dan admitted to me for the first time—indeed, the first time to anyone—that he was quite depressed toward the end of November 1978; that, in fact, he had long suffered bouts of despondency—perhaps as many as two or three per year, each lasting about a week, often without an apparent precipitant. During these spells he would become quite withdrawn and lethargic, have great difficulty sleeping, retreat to his room during the day, avoid answering the phone or even coming to the door; when employed, he simply called in sick. He took pains to avoid people because during these periods he found himself resentful and argumentative. That is, though usually he kept feelings hidden, during these depressive episodes he would have to avoid people lest his anger emerge—at that point he was not disposed to back down from any confrontation. Apprehensive about his potential for overt expression of hostility, he would simply keep to himself until the feelings passed.

There was another interesting feature to these depressions. A competent athlete, Dan ordinarily prided himself on keeping his body in "really good shape" with vigorous exercise and a nutritious, healthful, meat-and-potatoes diet. But when things were not going right, physical fitness would be abandoned in favor of a near-total lack of physical activity and high-sugar junk-food binges. He would lie around, gorging himself. The more he consumed, the worse he seemed to feel, responding to his growing depression with ever less activity and ever greater binging. Finally, these episodes would seem to run their course. He would pull himself together, start jogging, stop stuffing himself, and be rewarded by an improved mood, the reversal of his previous downward spiral.

But in November of 1978, there was no respite and no reversal. He was putting in a fifty-hour week as a supervisor, plus a minimum of twenty hours a week in his fast-food business. He rarely saw his wife; when he was home, she was out at the shop, and vice versa. Swimming, running, softball, and other valued recreational pursuits were now gone from his life. "There was simply no time, and even if I had the time, I didn't have the energy. Those last four weeks I gained about twenty pounds."

On November 10, seventeen days before the double homicide, he resigned his seat on the board.

"It seemed so futile. I either had to play the game or be on the short end of every vote. Arguments didn't matter. It didn't matter how hard I worked, I wouldn't get anywhere. I couldn't join them, I couldn't play it their way, so I resigned."

As was his habit, he consulted no one, but abruptly submitted his resignation letter to the mayor. In it he cited financial pressures as the only reason—although in our interview, he admitted that the controlling factor was really his disillusionment with the political processes of which he had become a part.

"Why didn't you say so publicly?"

"To have given the true reasons, the political reasons, would have meant more bad-mouthing. I didn't want to go out that way. Besides, it was my decision. Nobody else's."

"So there you were, on the outside again. How did that feel?"

"It felt great! After a year of all that pressure, it was all over."

Only it wasn't. Relief was followed almost immediately by feelings of despondency over having walked away from something, letting down his supporters and neighbors in the process.

Dan retreated into virtual seclusion while the press played. After several days, however, aides and supporters tracked him down, began working him over, and persuaded him that it was his duty to stay on. "They told me that I was the only one who spoke for them and that I didn't have their permission to quit."

On November 14 he made an appointment with the mayor and told him that he had changed his mind, that he wanted his letter of resignation back. Mayor Moscone replied, "Our political differences aside, Dan, you've always given me a fair shake. You are an honest man, and if you come back tomorrow, I'll have your letter for you." He promised Dan reappointment and as much as said so on television that night.

"Were you surprised? He was at the opposite end of the political spectrum from you."

"No. I expected that he would do that. He was the mayor, and I thought he would do the right thing."

"Sounds like you admired him."

"I respected him."

"They say his liberalism extended into his personal life . . ."

"It's nobody's business what people do in private."

I thought I had detected a recurrent theme—a familial parallel. "I'm told it wasn't always so private but he got away with it . . ."

Dan was not ready to tune into this possible echo of his feelings for his brother. "It was none of my business. The appointment was my business. He gave me his word. I knew he wouldn't let me down. That's what mattered," he explained, with a rare show of emotion.

But a few days later the mayor called Dan and said that "there was a problem"—one that could be overcome if Dan could provide his office with a visible show of support for reappointment. Dan made sure that this was forthcoming, that the letters and calls poured in; nevertheless, by the end of the week, the mayor apparently had pulled back from his previous promise. On November 20 the mayor's press agent announced that "the only one that [sic] supports Dan White for reappointment is Dan White."

Of course, this turn of events was devastating. (His sister Nancy reported to me that on the one afternoon he allowed her to visit him, she found him just sitting around in his bathrobe, utterly disinterested in her conversation and family matters. Preoccupied and apathetic, he sat unseeingly in front of the television, which he ordinarily ignored in favor of books, gobbling Twinkies, and gulping down Coca-Cola.)

Unable to sleep, Dan retreated to the living room couch so that his tossing and turning would not disturb Tina. Sleepless at night, he was fatigued and lethargic all day. He felt increasingly depressed, even dazed and confused. He had crying jags, became quite irritable, and wanted to be left alone. He stopped shaving and refused to go out of the house to help aides rally support.

(Tina reported to me that their sexual activity had stopped completely, that her husband wanted to be left by himself. Additionally, he instructed her not to bother cooking for him. His aide Marjorie also reported that during this period he underwent a personality change, becoming rude, sloppy, unsmiling, and inclined to swear.)

In Dan's mind, though, he was merely "stuck . . . part of me wanted to fight and get back my job but another part of me just wanted to be done with it and forget it. I decided to just leave it to fate. Staying in my room seemed the best way to do it."

On November 25, Sunday night, television reporter Barbara Taylor got through to him for "his comments on the fact that it was *final*—that he was not going to be reappointed"—the first definitive word Dan had received on the subject.

He slept not a minute the entire night. He paced, he sat, he stood up, he drank a six-pack of Coke, he lay down, he paced some more. At dawn Monday, around the edge of the windowshade he glimpsed the sun rising. Conflicting thoughts raced through his mind, too rapidly for him to follow any of them to conclusion. "So I figured I was just going to let whatever happens happen."

At about nine A.M. he took a call from Marjorie, who tried to stimulate his involvement. "Come on, Dan, we can turn this thing around."

"No," he said, and hung up. But the call got him to thinking. Perhaps he *hadn't* made enough of a personal effort. True, he had called the mayor on the phone several times without getting through, but if he personally went down to City Hall, surely the mayor would see him. By nine-thirty, he had decided to make a last effort.

Dan shaved, put on a suit and tie, and called Marjorie to pick him up (his wife having taken the family car). As he started to leave, he saw his gun lying on the desk, put it in his holster, and automatically dropped a handful of bullets in his pocket.

"You were going to see the mayor and for no particular reason wore a gun?"

"It had nothing to do with seeing the mayor. I'm an ex-cop. I often wore a gun. Supervisors Feinstein, Tamaras, Barbagelata, Nelder, and Francois carry guns. There was a rumor about a People's Temple hit squad coming to City Hall. Not even remotely was there the thought in my head of using it. I was going to try and get my job back. There was nothing else left for me to do."

Marjorie picked him up and, chattering away, drove him to City Hall. Dan half listened, replied in monosyllables. He felt great unease about a variety of things—not knowing what the mayor might do, a rumor that the mayor had avoided taking receipt of the very support he had asked him to supply, the repercussions of Jonestown.

(By contrast, Marjorie reported to me that Dan was hyperventilating, rubbing and blowing on his hands, struggling to hold back tears, was agitated and kept repeating, "I just want to talk to them—have them tell me to my face why they won't reappoint me. Do they think if they look me in the eye and tell me, I can't take it? I'm a man—I can take it!")

After arranging to return in about half an hour to take Dan to meet Tina after his appointment, Marjorie dropped him off in front of City Hall. Dan went first to the supervisors' private entrance but then, realizing that Marjorie had all the keys, instead entered by way of a large ground-level window often used as a door.

"Why didn't you just go around to the front?"

"I did. The security guard manning the metal detector always waves supervisors right around it. But this time there was someone I didn't know who probably wouldn't recognize me. I just didn't want an issue over carrying a firearm. I had enough issues to worry about. So I went through the side window. Lots of people who work in City Hall use it."

Dan headed upstairs to the mayor's office and asked the secretary in the anteroom if the mayor would see him. She checked with Mayor Moscone and told Dan that the mayor would meet with him in a few minutes. They chatted a bit until the mayor buzzed for his admittance.

The issue was immediately joined: Dan asked Mayor Moscone, "How are you doing?" and the mayor replied, "Well, *I'm* doing fine, but I'm not going to be able to reappoint you."

"I was stunned. Right away the thought starts going around and around in my head—I'm not going to get the job back—people are counting on me—what am I going to do?"

Dan tried to get the mayor to share with him the basis of his decision, pointing out to him that "I'm an honest guy, I work hard, I'm not lined up with any special-interest groups. Why would you not reappoint me?" But to the best of Dan's recollection, all the mayor did was repeat his previous statement, "I'm sorry, Dan, but I'm not going to reappoint you." Several times again Dan asked the mayor for his reasons but each time received none.

Finally, Dan fell silent, a leaden torpor settling over him.

"I felt deflated and limp. I got kind of flushed. My head was pounding, my face was hot."

The mayor put his arm around him and led him into a small adjacent room, saying, "Let's have a drink," and had Dan sit on a small couch while he poured for both of them. Then he asked, "What are you going to do now, Dan? Can you get back into the fire department?"

Dan's stomach knotted at the prospect of engaging in any personal discussion with the mayor. He rose from the couch, increasingly anxious, and started to pace.

The mayor began asking him about his family: "Can your wife get her job back? What's going to happen to your family now?"

"That last question hit me. I felt totally helpless, directionless. The mayor's voice faded out. I felt as if I were in a dream. I started to go out of the room. Then I turned around and took out the gun."

"Why?"

"I don't know why. It was like a reflex . . . I wasn't thinking . . ."

The mayor started to rise from his chair. Without a word, Dan began to shoot. He has no idea of how many shots he fired, no recollection of actually leaving the mayor's office or of reloading his gun. He then rushed down the hall. He had only one thought: "I've got to get out of here."

His next recollection is that of going through a door to the supervisors' offices. He saw Supervisor Harvey

Milk in his office and asked, "Harv, can I talk with you?" Dan entered the office, shut the door, and asked, "What the hell is going on? Why are you working against me? Why are you trying to keep me out of my job?"

At that point it seemed to Dan that Harvey was "smirking" and moving toward the door. Again he pulled the revolver, shooting Harvey Milk five times.

"I had no chance to even think about it. I remember how shocked I was by the loud sound in that office—like a cannon. Everyone came screaming out in the hall. I ran outside, saw Marjorie, got the keys, and ran down to the car. I had to get away."

As he drove down Van Ness Avenue, he saw a phone booth, managed to reach his wife, and arranged to have her meet him at St. Mary's Cathedral. From there they went together to the police department, where he gave himself up.

As these words are being written, Dan White is within hours of being released from the prison where he has served little more than five years for taking the lives of two highly esteemed men. Prevailing opinion is that justice was not served.

Certainly it was not, if one compares his penalty with the life sentence recently given a Texas man following a third conviction for mere possession of marijuana. On the other hand, the White jury was satisfied, as am I, that however heinous his offense, it was an emotional response rather than the product of deliberate rational thought—that White did not go to City Hall that morning with a conscious plan to hurt anyone.

White has long been engaged in a primal struggle "to belong," "do the right thing," and take charge of his life, but always, in the end, has been overtaken and directed by outside pressures, as he was in November of 1978. A second fundamental theme throughout his life has been his hypersensitivity to a real or imag-

ined lack of support—by family, superiors, community—coupled with an exaggerated self-reliance and pseudo-self-sufficiency as a defense against his fears and unmet dependent needs. At the time of the homicides, he experienced himself as very much alone, or at best, unable to utilize the help of those who were behind him, having never developed the ability to lean on others.

Clinging to the illusion that jumping back onto the Board of Supervisors would somehow rescue him from his psychic frying pan, emotionally drained and physically exhausted when he arrived at the mayor's office on November 27, he was utterly undone by Mayor Moscone's definitive and seemingly unreasonable act of pulling out from under him his only remaining hope of emotional support and self-esteem. The political brother he had counted on had let him down in a profound way. It felt as if the family had done it to him once more.

(Ironically, reappointment would have merely perpetuated those pressures that had already nearly exceeded his coping mechanisms, an exchange of one intolerable situation for another. By this time, however, any grass probably would have looked momentarily greener to him, so long as it was not of the field upon which he was then standing.)

With this last door suddenly shut and locked, White had no place to turn. Frozen out yet again, he broke apart. The granite crumbled. Moments later, the two men who had unknowingly inflicted a last terrible narcissistic wound lay dead.

I was not inclined to this view when I began my psychiatric evaluation, instead subscribing to the still-prevailing perception—of local journalists and pundits, none of whom ever personally examined the killer—that this was simply a political assassination. Certainly, Dan White is not "my kind of man": His politics are assuredly not my politics; his narrow, simplistic, macho view of the world anathema to mine. I suspected premeditated vengeance, right-wing paranoia, homophobia, a misguided sense of heroics. I looked for them. I prodded and poked. I couldn't find them. That is not to say that these elements were not there, but only that after a diligent search, I did not find them.

3

SUMMARY:
THE DISSOCIATIVE KILLER

SOLLY AND DAN are overcontrolled men who for years adamantly and sincerely denied their aggressive selves. Neither was aware of any hostility towards the victims. Roslyn was "a perfect wife"; Mayor Moscone and Supervisor Milk were "just doing their jobs." Solly's psychic structure allowed him neither to look honestly at what was happening in his marriage nor to leave it. He was unable to say, "This is unbearable. I love you, I need you, but I cannot live with you. I'm getting out." And although Dan initially tried to escape his psychic trap, he too overrode his instincts and flayed himself into trying to get back in.

That the rage of these two men was stubbornly disowned is not to say that it did not have continuing effect. Throughout their lives, neither could count on complete success in his struggle against the emergence of forbidden feelings. At times both would try unconsciously to dispose of some aggression by pinning it on others—portraying themselves as victims of aggressive behavior which did not in fact occur, save as projections of unacceptable aspects of themselves. At some level both felt guilty for having assaultive impulses; and they remained in punishing situations in an effort to absolve some of their guilt. Both were programmed with punitive consciences which told them "You can't quit, you have to stick it out, you deserve the beating you're getting."

An intolerable situation from which there appears to be literally no exit can precipitate a dramatic psychological escape in which the trapped individual's rational, controlling mind is briefly dissociated from repositories of angry feelings. Thus freed from control, unmitigated rage may execute a solution the conscious mind would otherwise reject. Though physical factors such as fatigue, insomnia, alcohol, drugs, and diet may contribute, this disconnection of intent from behavior is largely an involuntary mental process that usually strikes no more than once in a lifetime. In a highly repressed individual, out of touch with his feelings, desperation and wrath—unrecognized, long-festering, and unexpressed—can finally short-circuit an overloaded consciousness. A sudden, lethal eruption ensues.

In dissociation, the conscious mind goes blank. The unconscious acts in its stead, sometimes in a murderous manner totally at war with the killer's usual characteristics, behavior, and self-image. In this brief, bloody state of altered consciousness, a way out is at last secured.

Solly and Dan illustrate the multifaceted nature of homicidal dissociation. Both were complex men who killed for complex reasons. These were presented in detail at trial by myself and several other defense psychiatrists who were then questioned closely and meticulously by prosecutors during the course of lengthy cross-examinations. Reducing this scholarly, well-supported, carefully scrutinized testimony to "the sleepwalking defense" or "the Twinkie defense" does great injustice to forensic evidence, to psychiatric experts and attorneys who present it, and to jurors who wrestle with it conscientiously and ultimately choose to give it weight.

II

THE
POWERLESS
KILLER

Children raised with a modicum of respect and with some appreciation of who they are as individuals will grow into adults possessing some sense of personal power. Unfortunately, not a few children are brought up in homes where they are regarded as invisible or little more than biological extensions of their parents. Accordingly, they may reach maturity uncertain of their value as people, and suffering grave doubts about the degree to which they can influence the course of their own lives. Swept along helplessly by events, they lack the psychological means to move toward that which might make life worthwhile or away from people or circumstances regularly bringing them to grief. Feeling utterly without power of their own, they can become totally submissive to the pernicious will of others. Yet, paradoxically, when nothing else works, they may finally be moved to the use of lethal force. Even an emotional cipher—a virtual non-person—if sufficiently desperate, may find the strength to fire a gun.

4

A REAL MAN

"WITH MICHAEL I got myself a *real* man. He could even stand up to my father. The first guy I ever went with that I could really respect. Then we got married . . ."

Darlene had a strong sexual presence—an air of easy accessibility—perversely coupled with a fine-featured face of elegant loveliness that conflicted with her rough speech and debilitating lifestyle. Her full mouth drew lovingly on a cigarette. She exhaled the smoke as she spoke.

"Thanks for letting me smoke while we're talking, Doc. In your cell they only let you have five a day. I climb the walls—been smoking three packs since I was thirteen."

It was August and well over one hundred degrees in the small, central California jail, the taxpayers having seen no reason to reward the wrongdoers amongst them with air-conditioning. There Darlene was indeed sweating out her impending trial for aiding her husband, Michael, in the mutilation and murder of an old boyfriend.

Michael had been tried first, convicted, and just sentenced to life imprisonment. The District Attorney, now confronted by Darlene's insanity plea, had asked the presiding judge to appoint me to examine her prior to her turn in court. He could not see her claim of mental illness as in any way credible, but then, he admitted, he had never placed stock in such claims. What could I tell him about Darlene? Did she have a legitimate psychiatric defense and was a jury likely to accept it?

Darlene dabbed her face and neck with a tattered washcloth she had brought with her to the tiny interview cell. The blouse of her jail uniform was partially unbuttoned and she was braless. Doubtless her jailers disapproved but were themselves too enervated to care very much.

She smiled. "And they call this place the cooler! I can't get anyone to come visit. Not in this heat."

"Not even your father?"

"Especially my father. He does things *when* he wants, the *way* he wants."

"Sounds like he's pretty much his own man."

"Yeah, he's his own man all right. You don't mess with my father. Strongest, toughest guy I know. Don't say much, but there's no one like him. He's sixty, y'know, and in his bikini trunks he still makes all the other men at the pool look like pussies."

I had spent less than two minutes with Darlene and already had a sense that the key to her participation in a brutal homicide lay in her relationship with her father, and that she was ready—eager—to tell me anything about her life with him that I needed to learn. I began by asking her about her childhood with this taciturn, unyielding man.

She described his strictness with her, his only child. Often difficult, perhaps impossible, to please, he beat her freely for trivial transgressions.

"We fought all the time. Actually, *I* fought all the time. He'd just stand there, y'know. He wouldn't hardly let me do much—smoke, wear makeup, go out with boys. Not much of anything. Usually I did anyway. He'd find out, slap me a little, and make me stay in my room for a week. I'd go to school and come home for dinner and then I'd have to go back to my room. But by eight o'clock I'd be out the window, over the garage, and down with my friends."

"He never checked your room?"

"He'd usually polish off a fifth of bourbon by that time and be dead to the world. Oh, he caught me once or twice, beat the shit out of me. Mostly I got away with it. But I never did nothing in front of him, y'know. In front of him it was, 'Yes sir!' He'd just have to look at me."

"You were afraid of him—yet defied him. What kind of attention did you get when you behaved yourself?"

"I don't think he noticed one way or the other. I guess he took it for granted that I was going to be good. He wasn't much for compliments. But get out of line and you'd hear about it."

"Doesn't seem to me like your childhood was much fun. What about your mother—couldn't she soften some of your dad's harshness?"

"My mother?" Darlene smiled. "My mother didn't count for nothing. She just did as he said. He wouldn't never listen to her anyway. My father ran the show. My mother didn't matter."

"I suspect *no* woman mattered very much with your father."

"I don't know . . . my father had about two dozen truckers—*guys*—working for him, and it was the same there. They all did what he said. No arguments. Men run the world and my father runs men."

For Darlene, it appeared that maleness meant power and strength. Femaleness had little value and, thus, neither did she. Lacking a positive model in her mother and receiving little affirmation from her father, she sought and apparently obtained approval from neighborhood boys, making up for the emptiness in herself by pleasing men. By the age of seventeen she had been pregnant three times. Each time she miscarried.

"You had a lot of boyfriends?"

"Not actually boyfriends." She blew a few smoke rings. "I got laid a lot."

"I gather that after they had sex with you they wouldn't stay around."

"No. I guess they got what they wanted. But I didn't care either. They were just dumb kids."

"But Michael was different?"

"Yeah, he was different all right." She lit a new cigarette with her old one. "Maybe I should have stayed with dumb kids."

The Michael she described sounded like a young version of her father—physically strong, rigid, and authoritarian. "He kind of took me over. Told me how he wanted me to dress, how to fix my hair. He made me stop smoking."

"He didn't smoke?"

"Yeah, *he* smoked all right. It's just that he didn't want *me* to smoke. I smoked anyway. When he wasn't there. That's when we had our first big fight. He found my cigarettes and pushed me around."

"Did he do that a lot?"

"No, no he didn't. Only once in awhile. When he was shitfaced. Really shitfaced and on pills. Mostly, we balled a lot. At first."

"Your sex life was pretty good, then?"

"Yeah—till I got pregnant with Sammy. Then we got married. After that I noticed we would only get it on when he was really high on pills. Otherwise he seemed to have a problem getting it up."

"What kind of pills?"

"Mostly uppers. Black Beauties. Benzadrine. He ate lots of bennies."

"And you?"

"Oh, sure. Me too. By the time Sammy was born, I was keeping up with him."

"And drinking?"

"And drinking. Michael and I could put away a fifth together in one evening easy. He was on the road a lot and I wouldn't drink so much when he wasn't around. But I still did my share."

"And your share of uppers?"

"Yeah."

"Where did you get them?"

"Michael always had them. All truckers have them."

"Didn't all these pills and booze get in the way of your . . . doing the things you had to do?"

"Not usually. Not at first."

"Where was your son through all of this?"

"My mother took care of him mostly. What with me working."

"Where was that?"

"In the office of Tyler Cadillac."

"That's the dealership right here in town?"

"Yeah. It was a good job. I wrote up the sales contracts, answered the phone, did a little bookkeeping. The salesmen, they all treated me like I was a princess. Never been treated like that by anyone before. Those guys really know how to treat a girl right."

"What do you mean?"

"They'd take me out to a classy place for lunch, y'know? Or we'd go out after work when Michael was on the road."

"May I ask—did you have a romantic relationship with any of them?"

"What do you mean, a *romantic* relationship?"

"Well, what would happen when you went out with them?"

"You mean, would I have sex?" She paused. "Y'know, Michael doesn't know about this—yeah, I guess I balled all of them one time or another."

"Why?"

"They treated me good. They wanted it. And I was shitfaced a lot. But mostly because they treated me like a lady."

"What about Michael?"

"Yeah—well, he was getting pretty weird by that time. The sex was really getting weird."

Darlene then described her husband's use of sadistic fantasy to restore his flagging potency. Frequently the two of them would enact bondage scenes in which he would pretend to torture her and she would cry out in simulated pain. Or, lying naked in bed, they would fantasize a scene of torture involving a neighbor or friend. All of this was quite sexually arousing to Michael and would culminate in intercourse. Unfortunately, in time the arousal value of these enactments began to fade, and Michael turned to actual sadistic acts, first biting or slapping Darlene, later going on to hitting her more forcefully, tying her more tightly with leather straps, putting clothespins on her nipples, and finally, the last few times, lightly touching glowing cigarette tips to her skin.

"You enjoyed this sort of thing?"

"I hated it!"

"Why didn't you stop him?"

"I love him. He's my man. Y'know a man needs to get a hard-on in order to ball and these things gave him a hard-on."

"How long did this continue?"

"Where he actually hurt me? Only about two weeks. 'Cause then, he found something else to talk about. And he would get excited when he talked about this and didn't need to hurt me anymore."

"Which was . . ."

"We'd lie on the bed. Then he'd start to tell this story about murdering someone. Having sex with them and then murdering them. Then he'd get all involved in the details. Beating them, stabbing them. Blood everywhere.

Soon he'd really get turned on and we'd ball! He didn't need to hurt *me* anymore. So I went along with it. It was a lot better than getting beat up."

"But still it wasn't very good . . ."

". . . it was the pits. The only way I could stand it would be to get shitfaced. And I must have been eating—I don't know—maybe fifteen or twenty pills a day. With pills, things didn't bother me. But I needed a lot of booze to sleep, to relax."

"When was this now?"

"This would have to be early April. Because we killed Corky on the twentieth of April."

Darlene's relationships with men, and particularly with the two most important ones in her life—husband and father—were, to say the least, regrettable. But there was nothing thus far to suggest mental derangement. In any event, she had never directed violence at either of the two principal men in her life. Her drug and alcohol use certainly raised the question of mental incapacity, but so far as I could tell, her brain had adapted well to a daily chemical bath that appeared to have insulated her a bit, enabling her to function despite difficult circumstances. What was as yet unrevealed, then, was some recent singular experience or trauma that might provide the explanation for Darlene's uncharacteristically lethal conduct.

"Maybe I should interrupt you here and get you to tell me something about Corky."

"He was just this kid I used to know. A real nice guy. He used to work for my father too until he hurt his back. Michael knew him. He just lived alone. I think he got disability. I'd see him in town a couple of times a month. We'd stop and talk."

"You had a romantic . . . a sexual relationship with him?"

"Yeah, we balled a couple of times, y'know? No big deal. It was hard for him. Because of his back, and all . . ."

"You liked him?"

"Sure."

"But you killed him."

"I never wanted to—I never meant to do anything like that. It just sort of happened. Once it got started, it kept going."

"Can you tell me how it got started?"

Darlene lit another cigarette. She exhaled with a deep sigh; her face reddened and tears came to her eyes, dampening her earthy hot ambiance.

"Michael came home around five o'clock that Saturday. We just sat around drinking. We ate a lot of pills. I wanted to make supper but he said he wanted to ball. So we went into the bedroom. We lay down on the bed and he started this scene about Corky, y'know? Like we would be going to his house that night and be real friendly, ask about his back and all. Then we'd talk about his sex life. Corky was only nineteen. Even with his back, he always got it up. Michael liked to hear about that. Then we made up this plan where I was going to massage Corky's back, and when he wasn't looking Michael would hit him on the head with a hammer. Then—then we'd cut off his dick and his balls. We'd leave a lot of false clues and nobody would ever find out who did it . . . or what happened to Corky's dick. I know this sounds pretty sick. But this bullshit sure beat getting hit or burned.

"Then, Michael sat up and said, 'Let's really do it!' He wanted us to *really* go over there. He got it all figured out.

We'd wear old clothes because they were going to get bloody and we'd have to burn them. And we were supposed to bring over a little plastic Baggie for Corky's dick. We'd stop off at the store and buy a strange brand of cigarettes and leave them around to fool the police. Michael ran around and got our hammer and a knife and we got into the car and drove over to see Corky."

"And you went willingly?"

"I guess. I was pretty fuckin' high."

"You didn't try to talk Michael out of it?"

"You don't talk Michael out of nothing that he wants to do. He wanted me to go. I went. I didn't think we would really do anything. It was just part of Michael's make-believe scene."

"But you came to believe differently, didn't you?"

"Yeah. I guess by the time we got to Corky's house I knew Michael was serious."

"When you realized he was serious, what did you do?"

"I kept right on going."

They arrived at Corky's house at about nine P.M. Corky was surprised but glad to see them. They had a few beers. Darlene asked Corky about his back and he replied that it hurt him most of the time but that he was used to it. Darlene offered to massage his back. Corky took off his shirt and lay down on the rug in front of the sofa.

Darlene massaged his back for a few minutes, then told him she could get at his thighs and hips if he were to drop his trousers. "Michael don't mind," she told him.

"I rubbed him for a while. Michael was just watching and drinking. I knew that he had that hammer and the knife in his pocket. I told Corky to roll over onto his back so I could get the rest of his thighs and hips better. Corky was just lying there with his eyes closed and this dumb little smile on his face. I was massaging pretty high up on his thighs, close to his balls, and he started to get a hard-on. Then Michael got out of his chair and hit him on the head with the hammer. Nobody said nothing. Corky didn't know it was coming. Michael hit him again. Corky wasn't breathing. Then Michael cut off his balls and his dick and put them in the Baggie. We were careful to wipe all of the places we thought we might have touched. Then we took off and spent the rest of the weekend in the mountains and Michael kinda balled me with Corky's dick. We came back Monday. They'd never even found Corky yet. Then, at the end of the week they did. But they couldn't figure out who did it. We didn't leave no clues."

"But finally, you told the police."

"Yeah. I went to work Monday. I was sure they were going to find out. But nothing happened. I couldn't believe what we done. I was eating lots of pills. So was Michael. He was really getting weird, y'know? Wasn't showing up for work or anything. Two weeks went by and still the police hadn't found anything. But I started thinking, what if Michael got really fucked up and decided to cut me or something? Or Sammy? And I thought about it and thought about it. I decided I had to tell the cops. So I went over to my father's house and called them from there. And they came on over, but I couldn't get nothing out. I just couldn't tell them nothing. But I guess I musta said enough because they decided to take me down to the police station. I hadn't had anything to drink for about eight hours. I was outta pills. I was a nervous wreck. One cop said he had some bennies. We stopped off at a store and got a six-pack and I drank some beer and ate some bennies in the car. In the police car. And I told them what me and Michael had done . . ."

Darlene had described for me the overvaluation of masculinity and the relative powerlessness of the female in its most extreme caricature. Darlene had no sense of self, no value save that acquired by her connection to a male. This connection was often literal—the male sexual organ. Her husband too believed that the male genitalia were the repository for strength and power. When his began to fail, he and Darlene, doubtless aided by considerable drug and alcohol toxicity, stole that of another. Darlene, of course, realized that to do so meant killing her friend, yet violence was excitement for Michael and Michael was "her man." She existed only to make her man happy. In this, Darlene's thinking was profoundly disturbed and distorted. *But* it was most doubtful that any jury would find her legally insane.

In return for assurances that she would not face the death penalty, Darlene abandoned her insanity plea, pled guilty, and was convicted of first-degree murder. She is eligible for parole in 1993. She will be thirty-nine.

5

A GOOD DAUGHTER

THE CAROLINE ISLAND of Ponape is a verdant speck in the remote South Pacific, lying at a point equidistant between Hawaii and nowhere. Trees overhanging the unpaved roads bend toward you, weighted by their harvest of mango, papaya, breadfruit. The surrounding seas are still crowded with shrimp, lobster, and brightly colored fish. In keeping with their Polynesian origins, Ponapean women often go about topless. There are few sexual barriers—one simply follows one's heart, the 280 days of heavy annual rain providing ample opportunity to do so.

To stumble upon a nineteenth-century paradise so little troubled by civilization would be remarkable even absenting Ponape's secret: You need not leave the United States to visit it—Ponape, zip code 96941, is an American Trust Territory. The Stars and Stripes fly above its tiny administrative complex and on the corner sits the familiar blue mailbox. The visiting judge follows American rules of jurisprudence.

The Air Micronesia puddle-jumper deposited me at Ponape's airstrip on Wednesday. I would be obliged to remain on the island until its next flight, Saturday.

The island's single taxi bumped and jostled me down the rutted road past a number of shops and businesses (all American-owned) to the island hotel, where for seventeen dollars I secured a cabin built of banana leaves and bamboo. My bathroom, which had only three walls, opened directly onto the jungle, leaving my activities in full view of whatever creatures might have had an interest in them. There is as yet no term for privacy in the Micronesian lexicon. Regrettably, there is one for murder.

Fifteen-year-old Bobbie was free on bail provided she did not leave the island. Slight of stature, deeply tanned but unquestionably Caucasian, she arrived at her lawyer's tiny office for her psychiatric evaluation, looking bedraggled, beaten, and hopeless. During the ensuing two sessions she smiled but once: early on, when talking about her earliest recollections—a Hollywood childhood on a tropical island, undemanding classes, and easy movement between her father's American culture and her mother's Polynesian one.

Her parents' only child, she had lived on Ponape all her life. Mother had brought her into the spiritual and cultural innerlife and spirit of Ponape. Father took her with him to the outer world, particularly to the neighboring islands, to Guam, and occasionally to Hawaii. Though parsimonious with praise, during those first years he had managed to provide Bobbie with a sense of a strong, loving bond between them. Still, she was closer to her mother—"the kind of mom I would hope to be someday. We could talk about anything. She could listen to me in a way my father never did."

For the first years of their marriage, Bobbie's father depended rather heavily upon his Micronesian wife, and upon her family's financing and their influence on Ponape and the other Caroline Islands. But as his business prospered and expanded, the domestic balance of power shifted, and the tolerance and affection he displayed for his family decreased proportionately. English was the only language spoken in the home, and given his wife's limited facility with it, she was bound to lose any argument with her husband. More and more, he began trampling her with words, or, frustrated by her broken English, refused to talk to her at all for long periods.

"I really started feeling sorry for my mom," Bobbie told me. "I tried to fill up the holes in conversations, and to explain to him what she was thinking, her thoughts and vice versa. For awhile that really seemed to help— just being a kind of go-between helped them get along better."

Then, two years ago, for reasons at first utterly inexplicable to Bobbie, her father changed dramatically and her life fell apart.

"He didn't seem like he cared about us anymore. He was mad a lot, started wearing funky old hippy clothing and long hair, and using really gross language. He told me I was a lazy fucking bitch and if I didn't start doing better, he'd knock my fucking head into the ground!"

"Your father hadn't been one to use obscenities before?"

"No, never. Not that I ever heard."

"So it really bothered you."

"Yeah, but, I think I was more shocked than bothered —other things about him bothered me a lot more."

"Like . . ."

"Like, he just didn't care. He didn't seem happy with *anything* I did. He was away one week and Mom and I painted the whole house by ourselves and when he came home he didn't even look."

She paused.

"Anything else?"

No response.

"Did he ever do anything . . . improper?"

"You mean to me?"

I nodded.

"No. Oh, he always used to be in the bathroom when I was showering, but he's done that since I was a little kid. Nobody cares about that kind of thing around here. Another time he slapped my face really hard 'cause I wouldn't cut my hair."

I had guessed wrong. "The worst of it then was . . . ?"

". . . he treated my mom like dirt. Like a *slave*. He would dictate how she should dress and how she should cook and what we should eat. He would tell her what programs to watch on TV. He was always looking for a chance to put her down. You know—'How come there's a ring around the bathtub?'—blah, blah, blah."

"What did you think had happened to your father all of a sudden?"

"At first I didn't know. I couldn't imagine. I really tried to figure it out. I thought maybe it was our fault. Or maybe things were going bad at work. Then I started hearing things at school. The other kids began saying things, like teasing me about my father's 'new American wife.' "

"You mean he had taken another wife besides your mother?"

"Some kind of rumor like that."

"What did you do?"

"I stopped going to school. I'd leave the house in the

morning but I'd just cut. Finally they sent a note to my parents. My dad read it and started shouting at me as soon as I got home. He didn't care that I was missing school—only what people thought about *him*. He told me that he was embarrassed to have to work with other fathers who knew that his kid wasn't going to school—they probably thought I was a dumb shithead—and that I was chopping down the reputation he'd worked so hard to build, blah, blah, blah.''

"Did you ever ask him 'What's this stuff about your other wife?' "

"Not then. But about two weeks later I ran into him on the street with this woman who worked for him—Mrs. Kent. They were walking arm-in-arm. He just said, 'Hi, Bobbie,' and kept on walking. So I knew it was true. But I wanted to hear it from *him,* so a little later I asked him about it. He told me it was none of my business."

"What was your mother doing through all of this?"

"She didn't know exactly what was going on, either, but she was hearing things about Mrs. Kent where she worked. Ponape is pretty small. I heard them arguing about it one night and him denying everything. She accepted what he said—at least she seemed to. I didn't have the heart to say anything to her about it."

"It sounds awful—for you and your mother."

"I *hated* him for what he was doing. Several times I stood up to him and asked him why he was doing these things. He told me he wasn't doing a damn thing and to shut up."

"Then what happened?"

"I ran into them a couple of times more. He was spending less and less time at our house. I don't think he was giving my mom any more money. We were mostly living off what she was earning.

"Mrs. Kent had a couple of sons—she'd been married to someone before. They were working for my dad now, too. I saw them driving his jeep a couple of times.

"So by now, I wasn't going to say any more to him. I didn't speak to him and he didn't speak to me. But then one day I had some friends over—two girls—and he just told them to leave the house. I started to yell at him. I asked him why he was so mean, why did he have to spoil everything—and I knew he couldn't be so mean to me if he loved me. He told me that my girlfriends were whores and he hadn't loved me for ten years."

"Good God!"

"So I ran away. I told my mom where I was going and I moved in with my best girlfriend."

"Your mother continued to stick it out?"

"Yeah. She'd *never* leave him. But I know he was trying to get her to leave so he could get a divorce—on *his* terms. Then one day Mom found Mrs. Kent's picture in his wallet. She showed it to him and he told her, 'Yeah, she's my girlfriend.' "

"Bobbie, I can't imagine that your mom hadn't known all along . . ."

"Yeah, only now he was rubbing her face in it. Then he left for good. I'm sure he wanted *her* to leave, but she wouldn't go, so finally he walked out.

"When he left, my mom drank all the liquor in the house. I've never even seen her drunk before. She got really sick and ended up in the hospital. I met my dad there one day when I was visiting her. He told me that he had only married my mom because she had threatened to kill herself if he didn't and that he never loved her. Then he said that she was suicidal and he was going to have her locked up in the loony bin. And he did. He had her shipped over to that big hospital on Guam for psychiatric care."

"Was she suicidal?"

"She wasn't suicidal, just really upset. Especially that first day when he walked out and she drank all that booze. But he just wanted her out of the way. Then he took all the money out of the bank. He even took my money out of my account where I was saving for a Moped. I went by the house and I saw him and Mrs. Kent taking the furniture and all the things he wanted. Then he had the rest packed up and he put a padlock on the house."

"So your mother had no place to go?"

"Not really. She came back to Ponape after a couple of weeks and moved into my grandparents' house, but there were already seven people living there. She felt tremendous shame having to come back like that."

"And by now you felt . . . ?"

"Everytime I thought about what he was doing to my mom I would *boil* inside. I started wishing real hard that something bad would happen to him. But afterwards I would try and push out those feelings . . ."

"Block out your feelings?"

"Because he was still my father—so my mom and I had to deal with him."

But it was well-neigh impossible. There was no longer even a pretense of civility. Father would come to where Mother worked and badger her about signing the divorce papers he had had drawn up—which apparently left her with nothing. Undoubtedly now clinically de-

pressed, Bobbie's mother would leave work and return
to her parental home where she would isolate herself
until work the next day. She lived in dread of running
into her husband and Mrs. Kent, an event the size of the
island made almost inevitable. But she found no peace
at home either.

"He kept sending my mom threatening letters all the
time. Once he even sent her one of those vibrators
shaped like a man's thing and he wrote this real nasty
note telling her to use it until she got herself a boyfriend.

"He made a mess of my mom. I felt so sorry for her.
She was crying all the time now. Nothing I did could
comfort her. She was ready to agree to anything my dad
wanted. Anyway, all she had been holding out for was
some money for me until I finished school."

At this point, I brought the session to a close—because
of Bobbie's relative youth, I had decided to keep the first
interview short. Later on that day Bobbie was scheduled
for psychological testing to rule out any subtle underlying pathology or criminality. She responded to the idea
of being tested with some enthusiasm.

"Will I be doing the inkblot test? I read all about that
last week in *Psychology Today.*"

"I'm sure Dr. Berg will be happy to give you the inkblot test. How about coming back to see me at nine
o'clock tomorrow morning?"

That afternoon, I was able to interview Ponape's constable, Max Schaffer, who had known Bobbie and her
family most of their lives and who considered her father
something of a friend. Schaffer made no judgment about
the man but was aware of his promiscuity long before he
took up with Mrs. Kent.

"Extramarital affairs have never been much of an issue

on Ponape. What disturbed me was the way he would flaunt them, making sure that everyone knew. He'd always be introducing his girlfriends to other friends as 'my mistress.' "

Just as he would brag about his enormous income, his having purchased a more powerful radio, or his ability to consume the most liquor, it was the display of his apparent virility rather than the sex itself which seemed important to Bobbie's father. He became more immature and reckless with age and, by the time he had taken up with Mrs. Kent, had openly put many of his girlfriends on the payroll—to what end, the constable could only guess.

His ever greater devotion to puerile hedonism was paralleled by a growing disregard for his family. He began to talk about divorce to his friends long before broaching the subject with his wife, primarily because he was loathe to give up her connections. He came to ignore Bobbie in favor of Mrs. Kent's children, not even bothering to show up for his daughter's participation in the Micronesia Teen Beauty Contest.

"Did you ever talk to any of them about this, Constable?"

"It wasn't my place. Actually, neither parent wanted to hear. In a way, they both had an investment in the status quo."

The following day, Bobbie resumed her discussions with me, describing an uncharacteristically polite phone call she received from her father on February 22, asking her to come over "for a chat." When she arrived, Mrs. Kent opened the door and led her to him. He got right to the point.

"I've just received these papers from your mother's lawyer. They contain provisions for my continuing to support you until your twenty-first birthday. I think you ought to know why I'm not going to accept these provisions: You are not my daughter. Your mother and I adopted you when you were a baby. I have no ties to you."

Bobbie looked stricken as she repeated her father's words to me, but there were no tears—just an icy calm.

"It was like he had stabbed me in the back. It was the worst thing he could have done to me. It was like he pushed me out the door as an outcast, telling me, "You don't belong *anywhere.*" There was no reason for him to say that, to just . . . wash his hands of me like that. Just so that he could get out of paying for me till I finished growing up. And the way he told me, right in front of Mrs. Kent—why did he have to do that?"

Bobbie fled her father's house and went directly to her mother, who tearfully confirmed the truth of what her father had said.

"My mom was planning to tell me when I was eighteen. But instead—to find out *that* way . . . I think my dad wanted to break down my love for my mom, too, so that I couldn't help her and she would be all alone.

"Right then and there something had to be done. I didn't want to kill my dad, but I didn't want him alive anymore either. I couldn't stand any more of what he was doing. I decided if I wanted to be a good daughter and love my mom, I'd have to do something to my dad."

Bobbie easily secured the gun of her girlfriend's brother and was waiting at the entrance of her father's business early the next morning. She watched him pull up in his jeep, take some parcels from the seat beside him, and start down the path toward her.

"I know it all must have happened very quickly, but for

a few seconds there, I had all the time in the world. I kept shooting until the gun was empty. He was only ten feet or so away and I think all the bullets got him. It seemed like an hour between each shot . . ."

The psychological testing came back entirely negative except for some immediate situational depression. A second psychiatric report —obtained by the prosecution—read much like mine. The prosecutor offered Bobbie acceptance of a plea of guilty to manslaughter, no jail time, and two years of probation.

Bobbie is now in college at the University of Hawaii, studying psychology. Tuition is being paid from the same funding source that had underwritten her legal and forensic fees: her father's life-insurance policy. He hadn't gotten around to changing the beneficiary.

6
AN ENVIRONMENTALIST

I T WAS the last day of winter. I had left a week of chilling, unremitting California rain and fog, tree-toppling winds, flooding and mud slides, for the warm bright sunshine of Alaska and a meeting with a mass murderer. A computer programmer, he had, without warning or apparent reason, attempted to kill every resident of the tiny, isolated back county village in which he lived. He succeeded with five.

The seventeen survivors were staggered:

"He was always a gentleman—a polite, quiet man."

"We are a tiny, snowbound, peaceful community. We all know each other, help each other, but mind our own business. It just came out of the blue."

"I had invited him in for a cup of coffee. As I reached for a cup, something hit me in the right eye. I realized I'd been shot. Another bullet hit me in the neck. Then he said, 'Look, you're already dead. Please don't resist and I'll make it easy for you.' I asked him, 'What have I ever done to you?' He told me that I'd never done anything and kept on shooting. I just don't understand . . ."

Even the voluminous records forwarded to me from a mental-health clinic in Atlanta, detailing Paul's extensive psychiatric treatment as a youngster, replete though they were with documentation of extraordinary parental insensitivity, provided little by way of hints of or insights into his homicidal violence two decades later when he was thirty-seven. Nor was there anything in his detached, superior demeanor to suggest his capacity for the obscene anger and contempt for life necessary to kill so many individuals with whom he had no apparent quarrel. But Paul himself, sitting utterly at peace in the Fairbanks jail examination room, saw no puzzle. He patiently explained to me what he perceived to be self-evident:

"Human life just isn't very meaningful. There is no great loss to this planet if any one individual suddenly ceases to exist. Of course, I do care for the living and try to protect them. That is why I felt so strongly about protecting the environment and why I tried to stop those who would despoil it."

"The people you killed and the others you planned to kill—they were despoilers of the environment?"

"No, probably not. They were to die only as part of my larger plan to destroy the Alaskan pipeline—to stop the pipeline and its awesome, destructive effects. The pipeline was my target, my passion. Those people, regrettably—they had to be sacrificed along the way."

"I see . . . or rather, I *don't* see at all. I'm sure I'm a bit rigid on this, but I always find the going easier if I can begin at the beginning. Can we go back a bit? Let me hear how you developed your . . . unusual philosophy, find out more, if you will, about what your life has been like, and finally, how you arrived at your decision to do what you did."

"I will cooperate with you in any way I can, Doctor. I didn't want my family to find out about what I had done. But now that it's all over the news, the best thing I can do to save their face is to enable them to say I did it because I was out of my mind."

"Were you?"

"Certainly not." He smiled, mischievously. "But, of course, I wouldn't want to tell you your business. I must say, nonetheless, that it would be most convenient if you did find me insane. I would truly appreciate that. As a youth, I had a great deal of psychiatric treatment, you know."

"Yes. I've had the opportunity to review your records. I see that you, your mother and father, all received psychotherapy. What was that like? What was going on in your life that you needed treatment for so long—what was it, two years?"

"Yes."

He took out a pipe and lit it. "I believe I am a product of what you chaps call a 'dysfunctional family.' My parents had only one thing in common that I could see—a taste for dominance. I didn't realize it at the time, but I see now just how much energy they put behind controlling the other, controlling me, controlling everything around them. My father used the bulldozer technique. He was a developer, you know, and he would try and knock down other people and their ideas, replacing them with his own, just as in his work he flattened trees, even small mountains. Then he would put up buildings in their place.

"My mother was equally powerful by virtue of being a model mother, a model everything. You couldn't improve upon the ideal she projected. She was the prototypical immovable object to my father's irresistible force."

"And your position when these battles of the Titans took place?"

"I did my best never to get caught standing between them. I certainly couldn't stand up to them. I shudder to think what my life would have been like had they not exhausted themselves fighting each other and instead turned full attention upon me. As it was, it was bad enough."

"Many couples have horrendous fights and still have powerful positive bonds between them. Did you get the feeling that despite it all, they loved each other?"

"Love, hate. It's much the same thing."

"I don't follow."

"Passion is passion," he said, with studied dispassion. "They loved each other, they hated each other."

"Did you have a sense that they loved you?"

"They loved me . . . in their way. They loved me to be quiet around the house. They loved me to excel in school."

He did. Sometimes. One year, he would make dean's list; the next, almost flunk out. Socially he was a consistent failure.

"I was very shy. I didn't seem to have any of the social graces. Nobody listened when I spoke. The fact that I was brighter, better-read, than everyone else didn't help. I was miserable in high school, college was worse. In three years of college I had only one date, and I'm almost certain she accepted my invitation thinking I was somebody else."

"So you were always alone."

"Yes, that was the hard part. I didn't miss not having

sex. I would not have considered it a wasted life for never having had sex with a woman."

"Were there *ever* any close relationships?"

"I can't say that there were—not till I got married. Maybe not even then."

"So you studied instead?"

"No. I didn't have to study. I'm very intelligent, you know. I read a great deal, drank a lot of coffee—a *lot* of coffee."

"What was your field?"

"I had many fields. I played the fields. I couldn't get interested in anything really. The thought of devoting myself for four years to a disciplined formal course of study, to master a particular subject, any subject, seemed irrational. I could not imagine myself completing such an ordeal. I did settle on ecology for a while. Do you know what the science of ecology is, Doctor?"

"I think so . . ."

"The science of ecology is the study of how man's technology is upsetting the balance of nature and destroying the planet . . ."

"That's a somewhat more apocalyptic definition than the one I had in mind . . ."

". . . and given man's nature," he continued "a futile science. Therefore, I switched to computer programing so that I could do something useful while the world went all to hell."

Paul dropped out of school and for several years made a good living as a computer programmer, saving his money and then moving from the Southeast to Alaska, where he opened his own business.

"I wanted to go where the air and water were still clear, where there were still hills on which man had not yet set foot. I wanted to be part of the earth's quietude. I wanted to return to nature, to pristine beauty. The Gulf of Alaska would be my Walden Pond."

There, Paul at last met a woman—an Aleutian Indian —with whom he was comfortable. She moved in with him and several months later they were married.

But Paul was not psychologically prepared for a romantic relationship of any duration and soon found the bloom of sexual feelings for his wife as ephemeral as the Alaskan summer. Nor was the wilderness ready for computer programming. Within six months Paul lost both his new spouse and his business.

"I began to feel that my life—perhaps all life—was ultimately futile. My marriage was meaningless, my business failed, and even here in Alaska, I saw more and more corruption and contamination by oil money, by development, by tourists and hunters, by polluters of all kinds. If there is one thing I care about passionately, it's the environment, the animals and plants, the helpless creatures, the support system for all life. If it could be destroyed in Alaska, it could—and would—be destroyed everywhere. 'Why go on?' I wondered.

"I decided that I would not. I would leave this earth while there was still something left to leave, but do it in such a way as to accomplish in death what I could not do in life."

"Which was . . ."

"To make an unforgettable environmental statement: I would destroy the Alaskan pipeline. By sabotaging the pipeline, I would stop the flow of oil out and the flow of money in. I would bring a halt to the destruction and to the masses of people that money brought with it. At the same time I would preserve our oil for a future period when this country might really need it."

In the service of this grandiose scheme, Paul developed a plan to hijack a gasoline truck, set it ablaze at the last moment, and crash it into the particularly critical Pumping Station Number 12, demolishing it completely. In the dead of winter, the viscous oil flowing through the pipeline would then stop, congeal, and clog the pipe permanently along its entire length. At the same time, Paul would be consumed by the flames and intense heat, thereby ensuring that he would never be identified or in any way recognized as the perpetrator, thus sparing his family any embarrassment.

"What about your teeth and such things?"

He grinned and bared his teeth. "These aren't mine, Doctor. Ashes—that's all they would have found. Just ashes."

"What about the men manning the pumping station?"

"They would have been sacrificed for the greater good of mankind as a whole. One must choose between a few individuals, however innocent, and the public interest."

First, however, he had to arrange for his own disappearance, so as to be certain that he would never be associated with the pyromaniacal act to follow. On March 1, he embarked upon a plan to wipe out the entire populace—some two dozen people—of the town in which he lived, dispose of their bodies in a deep and distant crevice, and thus be assured that he would be assumed among the missing.

"Many of these folks had weapons, of course. This is real frontier out here. But in my favor was the element of surprise. After I killed everyone I planned to commandeer the mail plane that came every two days and use it to dump the bodies where they would never be found."

"What went wrong?"

"Well, for one thing, a .22 caliber pistol wound is not necessarily fatal, I discovered. I shot one fellow in the head from about twelve feet and it didn't even slow him down. He went for his knife. I got that away from him and did what I could but he got away. Then the mail plane started coming in. It was about an hour early. In Atlanta, we rarely got the morning mail before four P.M. but in Alaska, of course it has to come in early.

"One of the women got out to the airstrip before I did and waved the plane off before I could slay the pilot. I knew he could see some of the bodies lying in the snow and the police would soon be upon me. I still had time, though. I grabbed the snowmobile and headed over the tundra for the highway. I thought perhaps I might yet get to a gasoline tanker truck and carry out my plan—a lot of them run along that road. But I was still several miles from the highway when a police helicopter swooped down and fired some shots. I stopped the snowmobile and gave myself up."

All of this Paul told to me in a quiet, arch fashion, pulling periodically on his pipe. He saw no conflict between, on the one hand, his concern and compassion both for his family's sensibilities and for humanity as a whole (sufficient to want to protect its oil supply and its ecological environment), and on the other, his utter lack of concern for individual life—including his own.

"I never thought I'd have such a problem committing suicide, but I guess the fact that I'm still here suggests the possibility that I must be ambivalent, don't you think, Doctor? Nevertheless, I don't plan to be a failure all of my life. I believe I might be able to make my statement after all. I have some other ideas, some very clever ideas."

"What ideas?"

He puffed on his pipe and smiled with malignant cheerfulness.

"Isn't that for me to know, Doctor, and for you to find out?"

7
SUMMARY:
THE POWERLESS KILLER

I T IS ironic that feelings of utter impotence can force the assuming of the greatest of all power—that of life and death. Darlene, like her husband, felt empty, devoid of any ability to influence the course of her life. She saw herself as without value, except when driven by chemicals or "hooked up" to a source of male energy. She was no more able to resist her husband's murderous impulses than a lightbulb to reverse the direction of the electrical generator supplying it. In an act analogous to that of the mythical vampires, she and her husband attempted to sustain themselves by incorporating the symbolic life force of another male.

Less bizarre but no less desperate were Bobbie's feelings of impotence. Helpless to effect change in her father's gratuitous psychological brutality, she resorted to the ubiquitous tool of the powerless—the pistol.

Paul's powerlessness was more subtle. A failure in his own eyes, and beneath his arrogant facade, increasingly depressed and suicidal, his inordinate need for psychological restitution and power exceeded that which accrued to him in the real world, forcing the creation of a lethal drama enacted on a stage at last large enough for his grandiose fantasies.

Paul and the two women all illustrate the significance of emotional stress and disorder in the evolution of lethal intent, even where such mental disability fails—as it did in these three instances—to reach the threshold of legal insanity. It is highly unlikely that a jury would have given much weight to psychological factors at Darlene's or Paul's trial, given the nature of their crimes. In Bobbie's case, on the other hand, the prosecutor's understanding of, and sympathy for, the psychodynamics of her offense spared her ever having to face a jury or a jail cell. Paul, by contrast, will have much time to contemplate and perhaps improve his prison environment, having been convicted of murder and sentenced to five sentences of one hundred years, to run consecutively. He will not be released before the year 2484.

III

THE
PSYCHOTIC
KILLER

Psychosis is a state of severe mental and emotional disorganization, characterized by, among other things, the replacement or distortion of reality by delusions and hallucinations. A psychotic may not see or hear the same things others do, and can have a quite bizarre notion as to the meaning of the activities around him and of his own acts. He may thus commit the most heinous offense, convinced that he is performing a valuable and socially approved service. When he recovers from his psychotic episode, he often will have little recollection of what he has done—and, indeed, find it as extraordinary and unacceptable as does everyone else.

Such episodes are rarely single, isolated events. Afflicted individuals usually have an extensive history of psychotic attacks (usually without criminal behavior). Though they may also enjoy many years of normal life during remissions, without therapy they can be expected to manifest psychotic thinking and behavior again in the future.

Psychosis is perhaps the ultimate psychological symptom: escape from reality. When all efforts to cope with one's environment and inner self have failed, the only step left, short of suicide, is to exchange one's real world and identity for something less threatening, however incredible this new arrangement may be. There are people for whom conducting a fantasized Napoleonic war is less stressful than doing daily battle with an all-too-real computer. Even imaginary communists or the very devil himself can be a more tractable opponent than the ghosts of one's own childhood.

8

FOR THEIR SAKES

MY ANSWERING SERVICE put the District Attorney's call through to my home.

"Doc—we just arrested this woman who poisoned her two teen-age sons. Can you see her?"

"The boys are dead?"

"Yeah."

"Awful!"

"Yeah. They've been dead about a day. She wanted to talk about it and I think she'd better talk about it to you."

"When do you want me to see her?"

"Now. Once we get her to the jail—you know what happens . . ."

Often what happens is that the truth gradually gets lost, buried, or distorted. Just after the commission of a crime, almost all perpetrators have a clear recollection of what they did and why, and often want to get it off their chest. It is far easier to gain understanding of how it happened that someone has killed if you talk to him immediately afterward: Several weeks later he will have begun to build defensive justifications or even entirely repress what was done; or perhaps he will have made contact with a lawyer whose "theory of the defense" (which may stand a considerable distance from the reality of the offense) requires that the killer "change his story" or remain entirely silent.

A District Attorney is himself less dedicated to a pure search for psychological truth than to acquiring an understanding of the killer's actions sufficient to determine the appropriate charge, and, if he anticipates an insanity defense, to getting a psychiatrist he trusts on the scene before the accused closes over or is silenced by legal counsel. The District Attorney knows further that "his" psychiatrist will have great advantage over a court or defense psychiatrist who may not become involved until months later and who thus will have the difficult task of reconstructing a distant event. At trial, whose testimony is more likely to be accepted than that of the doctor "who was there"—almost at the moment of death?

Within minutes of his call, the District Attorney and two sheriff's deputies arrived with Gladys. After quick inspection reassured the deputies that the premises were secure, they removed her handcuffs and allowed me to escort her into my office.

She was a fortyish woman in housecoat and slippers, with a sad face that managed to be at the same time both gaunt and puffy. Her eyes were swollen into slits from hours of weeping. She wore no makeup and her hair had not been brushed for several days. She was palpably depressed, sighed frequently, and spoke very slowly, with great effort.

"I don't know why they had to make those handcuffs so tight. Can you imagine me fighting off two deputies and trying to get away?"

"I suspect it's a routine procedure, Gladys. But I'll ask

them to leave them a little looser if they put them back when we're done. They probably will, you know."

"Yes." She sat silently for several minutes, rubbing her wrists. "I'm in a lot of trouble. I did a terrible thing. But I *had* to do it . . ."

"Gladys, before you say more, I have to explain to you that the District Attorney has asked me to speak with you . . ."

"*I* want to tell you what happened . . ."

"Yes, that's fine. I want to hear what you have to say. But you must understand that, though I am a doctor, in my capacity today I must learn all I can about what you did, as does the District Attorney, and I will be telling him everything you tell me . . ."

"I've already told him . . ."

"Well, I will tell him again what you tell me, and somewhere down the road I might be called to trial to give testimony and that testimony might be used against you."

Psychiatrists working for the state—at all times but particularly at this stage in a criminal prosecution—have a primal obligation to make clear to the defendant the purpose of their examination. Though not adversaries, neither are they there to provide treatment; the examination is as much a legal as a medical process, performed to obtain information from the defendant which will not necessarily leave him in a favorable light and with which he may be confronted at trial.

"It's all out in the open, Doctor. I have nothing to hide."

"Be that as it may, let me emphasize to you that just because they brought you here to my office doesn't mean that you have to speak to me. You don't have to say a word."

I then read her the Miranda warning advising her of her right to silence and to an attorney.

"They read that to me before."

"Well, I just want you to understand that it applies here too."

"Doctor, I want to tell you anything you want to know."

Gladys began to tell me about herself. By her fortieth birthday, she was on her own, seemingly secure; she made a living by buying old Victorian houses, restoring them while she lived in them, then selling at a profit and moving on to the next. With her were two bright and successful teenage boys who would soon be out of the home and in college. Yet after considerable and careful deliberation, she decided that she and her sons had to die.

"The world has become a terrible place, Doctor. There is so much violence, pollution. We live under a constant threat of nuclear annihilation. My own life didn't seem worth much under these conditions. And were I to go—if I committed suicide—who would look after my sons? I just couldn't leave them orphans—without a home. No family. The stigma of their mother's death by suicide hanging over them—I felt so guilty. How much could these boys stand, finding their mother dead?"

"I don't understand, Gladys. I know things certainly could be better on this planet, but to want to die because of it, and kill your own children—maybe we'd better stop here for a moment and go back a bit. I think I'd understand better if you would tell me a little bit about your-self, your background, and how you got to be the person you are."

Gladys described to me a childhood perceived as exceptionally happy, despite her father's history of enormous mood swings, till about age eleven, when financial adversity compelled the family's moving in with her mother's austere, stern parents. Their strict ways dominated the household:

"It was *their* house. I had to obey *their* rules."

She held the move against her parents for many years. Her childhood was then further marred by "much tragedy—my brother was disfigured in a fire. My sister's fiancé drowned."

Hypersensitive to criticism, she was "always trying to please." Such dedication invariably obtained her good grades, and following high school she attended Utica State Teacher's College in upstate New York. The sudden freedom of being away from home was apparently too much for her—she reports that at age twenty she "went out of control and flipped," and required hospitalization for some months as a consequence of a suicide attempt. Between bouts of melancholia she was filled with boundless energy and confidence, graduated college, taught school for a time, and then worked briefly as a stewardess for Pacific Southwest Air Lines. Her job enabled her to see other parts of the United States; like so many others, she found she preferred California and decided to settle in Los Angeles.

There she obtained a teaching position and shortly thereafter married. The marriage went well. She had two healthy sons in rapid succession. Then her husband drowned in a swimming accident; the following year her father committed suicide. "I think I cried every day after, for almost a year."

In the early Seventies she left southern California and its tragic associations in favor of a small town outside of San Francisco, where she reports that her own health "broke down. I had to have lung surgery for a collapsed lung. Afterwards I spit up blood and pus for months. My breath smelled something foul. I was always underweight. I felt unclean. I caught pneumonia several times."

Her fragile physical condition convinced her to give up teaching and, indeed, much of her social life. Instead, she turned her energies to the rearing of her children, while she supported herself, them, and her aged mother with her home-renovation business.

Several years ago, however, in a burst of unbridled optimism, she took on several houses simultaneously, certainly more than she could handle comfortably. Shortly thereafter, her mother suffered a stroke and died.

Gladys was overwhelmed. Euphoria was again displaced by profound depression. She dissolved a bottle of barbiturates in some milk, drank about half of it, and gave the rest to her sons.

"They thought it tasted a little funny, of course, but they never suspected anything. But I didn't have enough pills. I was practically in a coma for three days, but the children were hardly affected at all. That left me with something else to worry about, something else I had to live with—that I had tried to kill my children, and that I wasn't a good enough daughter to my mother when she was alive."

The following year she was again hospitalized for several months during a protracted period of despondency that followed the end of a love affair. She felt better at the time of her discharge but seemed to have lost much of her enthusiasm for fixing up houses. Her children, now quite independent, required little maternal care. Thus, she had nothing to keep herself busy and, in her words, "even lost my identity as a mother."

Approximately one month ago she began to ruminate about taking her life, hesitating only because she feared that her suicide would stigmatize her children, and that, given their strong religious beliefs, the immorality of it would be more destructive to them than the actual loss of their mother. The only way, therefore, that she could condone taking her own life would be to first take that of her sons. This she had to do in a manner that would neither cause pain nor raise their suspicions. She decided once more to try sleeping pills.

"This time I had enough barbiturates. Do you know, Doctor, that I was able to get three hundred and sixty capsules of barbiturates over the phone?"

"How on earth did you accomplish that?"

"First I called Doctor Wilson. He didn't even need to see me. The boys had been to him for some orthopedic problems, so he knew them. I told him that we were going away for a month's drive through the Northwest and could not sleep easily in motels—could we have some barbiturates? He gave us a month's supply."

"Over the phone?"

"Over the phone," she sighed. "Then I called my gynecologist. I told him the same thing. He phoned in a prescription for another hundred and twenty pills. The next day I called him and told him I dropped them in the toilet. So he prescribed a hundred and twenty more. When I get depressed I get really sly. And do you know —he was the one who had prescribed the pills four years ago when I tried to commit suicide. But I guess he forgot about that."

"Weren't the boys suspicious, especially since you tried it on them before?"

"They never knew that I did it to them before. They had no memory of it. They just went to sleep. Then they woke up. I never told them. They were always very dutiful, obedient boys. When I told them they had to drink this for their health—that it was medicine to protect them from some hepatitis that was going around—they drank it. They said, 'To our health, Mom.' But they didn't want to die. It took them two days just to go into a coma. Even with all that barbiturate in them. Finally, I had to smother them. I put plastic bags over their heads. The pills took so long that I knew I couldn't use them on myself. Someone would always be phoning or coming to the door. I figured they'd get to me before I died. So I decided to jump off the Golden Gate Bridge. First I stopped at Zim's to get a hamburger. I hadn't eaten in three days and I didn't want to faint before I got to the bridge. While I was there I met another real estate lady. We talked about real estate. Real estate was booming. She never asked me about my boys. That was a good thing. By then, I didn't know what to do. I couldn't even think of what to put in a suicide note. So I went back home and called the church elder, thinking he could help me, but all he did was call the police."

"It doesn't appear as if you've ever gotten the help you've wanted."

"Plenty of people have tried to help me but it never did any good."

She stood up and began to pace. "I guess I've been thinking of suicide ever since I was a child. I remember lying on the couch in my grandparents' house, almost catatonic. Then I would go away, maybe out in the country, and I'd feel better. I thought the fresh air made me feel better. Now I realize that the further I ever got away from them, the better I'd feel. I made my first suicide attempt when I was twenty-one. With pills. I've tried a dozen times now—look at all these cuts on my wrist—I blew it a dozen times, so I guess I'm never going to succeed. One time I got into the bathtub and then dropped two radios in the bath with me. Nothing happened. One radio just went 'pfsst,' the other kept right on playing. Under the water. It still works. I still have it. Zenith used to make wonderful radios, now everything's Japanese. Another time I breathed in the fumes of Clorox and Sani-Flush together. I read where a woman just breathed in a few breaths and died right away, so I did it for two weeks and I thought my nose was going to fall off but nothing happened to the rest of me except that I cured my sinus problem—it hasn't given my any trouble since."

The last few moments, Gladys had begun speaking faster and faster, her thoughts becoming packed and jumbled together. Her depression had suddenly lifted. She became animated, elated, an enthusiastic raconteur. Fragments of past events crowded out the death of her sons in her brisk switch from despondency to mania.

What I was seeing at that moment in my office fit the history Gladys had given me, diagnostic of the manic-depressive syndrome, wherein the sufferer bounces back and forth between, on the one hand, near-immobility, irrational pessimism, and despair; and on the other, frantic ebullience, grandiose self-confidence, and feverish hyperactivity. Her father's reported mood swings and suicide suggested the condition as a family trait; and while certainly Gladys had enough tragedy in her life to justify her considerable despair, her emotional lability— her overreactions to life's events—made certain the diagnosis of an intrinsic defect in her psychic thermostat.

The middle ground eludes such people. A whirlwind of energy, accomplishment, and euphoria while high, when at the bottom of their cycle, they view the world through the refractive medium of their unmitigated despondency, and it seems to them an intolerable place. When their melancholia again lifts they are carefree, blind to any problems or risks, and will drive through life at ninety miles an hour, convinced that they can hold the road, no matter how sharp a turn it may take.

Gladys was tried and found to be insane because of psychotic depression at the time of her offense. Today she sits in a locked ward of a state mental hospital, awaiting restoration of her sanity. Much of the time she is well and her mood is level, but on each occasion of her annual sanity hearing she has become either markedly manic or depressed. Thus, ten times to date, she has again been sent back to the hospital as "not yet recovered."

9

TWO HEARTS BEATING AS ONE

Y OUR HONOR: On July 16, 1983, pursuant to an order of the court filed July 1, 1983, I was privileged to perform a psychiatric examination of Fermi Nafi for the purpose of determining his mental competency to stand trial for murder. He is charged with the shooting death of his girlfriend, Tammy Brown, in their apartment on May 15, approximately two months ago. I understand that his attorney has asked that the court terminate all criminal proceedings against his client and remand him to a mental health facility on the grounds that he does not have the mental capacity to understand the charges, participate rationally in court proceedings, or assist in the preparation of his defense.

Past History (obtained with difficulty from defendant, whose narrative was inconsistent, rambling, and tangential, and whose thought processes were often fragmented and illogical):

Mr. Nafi was born thirty-one years ago and raised in Cairo. He described both parents as loving people who treated him well—as a "special kid"—and his childhood as a happy one. He attended school until age fourteen and then worked with his father, a contractor; discharged his three years' military obligation; rejoined his father; and then, at age twenty-six, fulfilled a lifelong ambition by emigrating to the United States.

Upon arrival, he experienced substantial culture shock —a longing for familiar faces, and difficulty with language, employment, and culture. He found the shabby neighborhood where he could afford to live a fearful place. He felt alone, yet was afraid to go out and meet people or immerse himself in American life. Self-esteem fell further when twice he failed his citizenship test because of an inadequate ability to read English. Nevertheless, as months passed, by dint of what he characterizes as hard work and unremitting honesty, he was able to obtain employment and ultimately rise to the position of housepainter. Earning eleven dollars an hour, he purchased a car and obtained more congenial living quarters.

Mr. Nafi states rather proudly that he has always been very sexually active but never had what he would describe as a serious girlfriend until his relationship with the victim, twenty-one-year-old Tammy Brown, which began early in 1981. He states that she was "just as if I had ordered her from a catalog—perfect in every way." She moved in with him in May and for almost two years they were what Mr. Nafi describes as "inseparable," "soulmates," "twins."

Then, on February 5, 1983, Ms. Brown had to move from their apartment in order to return home to take care of her mother, who had been stricken with cancer. Mr. Nafi pleaded with her not to leave—"Tammy knew I would die if she left"—and was utterly unable to accept her reassurances that she wasn't actually leaving *him*, but simply had to attend to her mother.

After briefly experiencing Ms. Brown's absence as nothing less than—to use his words—"the tortures of hell," it began to feel to him as if she were not really gone at all, but still there living with him. I wish to make it clear to the court that Mr. Nafi was not speaking *figuratively*. He felt that Ms. Brown was often very much at his side, watching TV, lying in bed with him, etc. Whenever he made himself tea he would brew her a cup as well. He would light two cigarettes, get her a Coke, and so on. His experience of Ms. Brown's literal presence continues—at least to some degree—to this very day.

Apparently, however, these hallucinatory responses to his loss did little to stem its effects. He became increasingly despondent, lonely, and tearful. He called Ms. Brown several times a day and begged her to return, but she could or would not—her mother was clearly terminal and Ms. Brown did not want to leave her alone for any length of time.

Mr. Nafi listened to her explanation but it did not register. He only knew what he felt—that Ms. Brown was moving further and further from him. Their occasional weekends together only made her ever-longer absences all the more poignant, all the more painful.

He states that in the weeks before Ms. Brown's death, alone and depressed, he felt increasingly worthless. "I just wasn't good for anything anymore. I lost interest in everything." By early April feelings of despair had devolved into suicidal thoughts, which soon solidified into a definite plan—he bought a handgun and was close to the act itself. He had in fact just written a suicide note, when, on May 15, Ms. Brown arrived to spend the night with him, took off her clothes, and got into bed with the expectation that they would make love.

He could not. He was in turmoil.

Then, at the last minute, after wrestling with the question "Should I, shouldn't I; should I, shouldn't I?" he brushed aside Ms. Brown's assertions that she would always love him, broke free of her embrace, reached under the pillow for his gun, and fired—at her. He then turned the gun on himself but reports that "something mysterious" happened to all the bullets. "A strange force took them. They were gone and I couldn't find them." He then attempted suicide by repeatedly stabbing himself in the chest, aiming for the heart. He states that there was blood everywhere but he didn't die—in his view, because of God's intervention.

This narrative notwithstanding, and in the face of subsequently being told repeatedly that Ms. Brown had died instantly, Mr. Nafi does not believe that she is dead.

"I will not believe it until I visit her at the cemetery. I know that I am not a killer because I don't believe in killing anyone. And the coroner is lying—I shot her only three times, not five. I remember everything."

As he spoke of his last night with Ms. Brown, many of his sentences embraced mutually exclusive ideas. For example, he would begin by speaking of her as if she were still alive "somewhere," but in the next breath he would tell of how "her death was a suicide for both of us." At one moment, Ms. Brown seemed only a vivid memory; at another, he spoke of her as if she were there in the flesh—as if he saw her beside him and could converse with her. By his increasingly delusional logic, given that Ms. Brown was alive and real to him, then obviously he could not have shot her, despite his having admitted to me just a moment before that he had.

MENTAL-STATUS EXAMINATION

With the defendant's history completed, I next performed a mental-status assessment—a kind of psychological X-ray—of the defendant's mind as he sat there before me in the jail interviewing room. In this portion of the interview the focus is less on the substance of *what* the subject says than on *how* he says it—for instance, what he *doesn't* say—his perceptual apparatus, thought processes, feelings, and behavior.

Does he hear and see the same things the rest of us do? Do his ideas hang together tightly or loosely? Is memory intact? What capacity has he for abstract reasoning and for judgment? What sort of emotions does he display? Are they appropriate? Any unusual behavior?

On this day, Mr. Nafi presented as an intense, darkly handsome, well-groomed young man who comprehended most questions in a surface way and replied with what appeared to be absolute candor. There was a language problem but it was not disabling.

Perception

Mr. Nafi was oriented to time, place, and person and was alert to his surroundings. There were moments when he appeared distracted by hallucinations.

Mentation.

Mr. Nafi's narrative was logical and coherent as long as the inquiry was carefully structured and he was called upon to provide only brief answers. When given open-ended questions and the opportunity to speak freely, however, his narrative became cluttered with inappropriate references, delusions, religiosity, and a clear loosening of associations. Typically, he rambled off the point into non sequitur:

> "I don't know why I killed her, so I couldn't have. God has said so. Suppose we both die—then what's going to happen? I'm worried about who's going to pay your salary, Doctor—I know you are coming here to help me and I want to be sure you are paid. I also want you to know that all I did was love her —that's all I did—and that's all that I wish for. Why did her mother have to get sick?"

Most striking was the perseveration of his thinking that he was legally blameless for Ms. Brown's death, that shooting her "was a mistake or something—how could I intend to kill someone who was my whole life?" He was particularly indignant about a statement attributed to the prosecutor that he had shot her because she was going out with other men; Mr. Nafi insisted that the prosecutor's statement was the first he had heard of such a thing and it was not possible—"She would never do that." He maintained that hers was not a permanent departure, that they had regular contact over the phone and frequent loving visits as well. He pointed out that she was naked in his bed at the time he shot her. His only thought at the time was "I didn't want to live anymore. By not having her around I had lost a part of *me.*" Consequently, he was ready to "join God"—with whom he had long had a relationship that seemed more pathological than spiritual to this examiner. (In my clinical experience, most people who speak regularly to God are devout; most people to whom God regularly talks back are psychotic.)

Memory, both immediate and remote, appeared sound, though he would fix on bizarre and irrelevant details, making it difficult to test recollection with precision.

There were moments when he seemed perfectly rational, but for the most part he was not: His understanding of the criminal charges and what might consequently happen to him fluctuated accordingly. Overall, his grasp of his possible legal defenses was tenuous, minimal, and distorted. He refused even to consider the possibility of severe penalties.

Affect (Emotionality)

Mr. Nafi was somewhat depressed, but admitted to feeling a good deal better since starting on Tofranil, an antidepressant prescribed while he was in the hospital. He did not seem the least bit anxious about his forthcoming trial. His defense, as he saw it, was simply: "I've always been a responsible and honest person." This, in his view, should constitute sufficient proof as to his innocence of homicide.

He denied suicidal thoughts at present, explaining that "It wouldn't work—I did my best five times. I guess God wants me to live."

Behavior

Behavior was appropriate throughout.

REVIEW OF RECORDS AND
INTERVIEW WITH COLLATERALS

1. At the time of his arrest, while being transported to the General Hospital, the defendant told arresting officer *Jack Hartley* that he and the victim had lived together in his apartment for two years. On February 5, they broke up but agreed they would see each other on weekends. The weekend before last, the victim broke their usual date. This last weekend, during which the victim stated she had been seeing another man, Mr. Nafi "decided we should die together."

He told Officer Hartley that he regarded himself as guilty of having taken a life, had never wished to kill anyone before, but could find no other way out: "I decided to take my beloved with me. After she left my whole world went dark . . . the reason I killed my girlfriend, Tammy, was to be eternally together and I believe in this. I hope they will put us in the same coffin."

2. Examining Mr. Nafi at the time of his admission to the General Hospital, *Dr. Rudolph Schmidt* found "a large knife wound penetrating the chest wall and pleura within fifteen millimeters of the heart. The patient is suffused with suicidal and other aberrant preoccupations, is grandiose, lacking in insight, is delusional, and acutely depressed."

3. The *preliminary hearing* transcript is significant for the presence of Mr. Nafi's frequent verbal outbursts—largely non sequiturs that strongly suggested an emotional state that made it difficult for him to observe the usual court formalities or apprehend the significance of what was taking place.

4. I conducted a telephone interview with Mr. Nafi's

friend *Cathy Bunnion*. She reported that the defendant, of whom she was almost the only friend, was, in her words, "often paranoid"—quick to imagine slights where none existed. Sometimes things he said sounded crazy to her, but she was never sure if these reflected a peculiar deadpan humor or if he just had problems expressing himself in English.

He stated to her that it was *he* who had asked Ms. Brown to move out; however, at the same time, he was quite jealous over the notion that she might well be dating other men. He often expressed the feeling that she was "using him" during their evenings together, when he would spend fifty or sixty dollars on her, only to see her then go home to her mother. Yet, he helped her with the move. He did not date others, seemed dependent on Ms. Brown, but could not make the relationship work. This was a source of considerable stress for him. About a month before the shooting he told Ms. Bunnion, "I am going to blow my brains out." Over the next few weeks, he became increasingly eccentric and preoccupied with religion.

The day after the shooting, Ms. Bunnion visited him in the hospital and found him quite psychotic—"further out" than he had ever been before.

5. I conducted a telephone interview with Mr. Nafi's neighbor *Gilbert Smith*. Mr. Smith reported that Mr. Nafi was very upset after Ms. Brown had left him, that he was very much in love with her and couldn't stand what was happening. Mr. Nafi indicated that he didn't want to lose Tammy as he had lost another girlfriend several years before. Then, almost in the same breath, he insisted that Ms. Brown had not moved out but was in fact living with him.

Mr. Nafi stated on about six occasions that he planned to kill himself. He also stated at one point—using the word "guess" or "maybe"—that he was going to kill Tammy. Later he recanted, stating that he couldn't hurt anybody. Often he said things that made no sense whatsoever, especially in the weeks just prior to the shooting.

6. I conducted a telephone interview with *Rudolph Eaton,* brother-in-law of the victim. Mr. Eaton described the defendant as increasingly dependent upon Ms. Brown, who, though not withdrawing love, was becoming increasingly independent of him, to Mr. Nafi's growing despair. He never made any threats against her that he could recall, but often talked about how he could not live without her, and that suicide was something "everyone should consider." Sometimes he spoke as if Tammy were literally there with him, when Mr. Eaton knew for a fact that she was at her mother's home.

PSYCHIATRIC DIAGNOSIS

Functional psychosis—possibly *psychotic depression* but more likely *schizophrenia.*

CONCLUSIONS

Fermi Nafi is clearly psychotic. His commerce with reality is variable and uncertain. He has only an intermittent, fingernail grasp of the charges against him and the possible penalties that he faces. Perhaps he could participate, after a fashion, in the court proceedings, and in a peculiar way might very well be his own best defense witness, but there is enough clinical data to support his attorney's conviction that he simply cannot adequately represent

Mr. Nafi in his present state. In sum, the defendant's comprehension of the charges against him and of the significance of his own criminal acts; his ability to participate in the court proceedings, to appreciate the possible penalties, and to cooperate with counsel—all are in great flux but generally marginal. His mental disability is most likely sufficient for him to be found incompetent to stand trial within the meaning of Section 1368 of the Penal Code.

The judge determined that Mr. Nafi was too deranged to make much meaning of any trial and had him transferred to the state hospital for three months of psychiatric treatment. At the end of that time, I was ordered to reexamine him. I detected residuals of his schizophrenia, but found him now psychologically fit for his day in court.

The trial went forward.

Fermi had a few outbursts, and insisted, against his lawyer's advice, upon testifying at length on his own behalf; otherwise, the trial was not remarkable. The jury believed the defendant to be severely disturbed at the time of his criminal act but decided that he knew enough about what he was doing and had sufficient control over his conduct to warrant conviction for second-degree murder. He was sentenced to life imprisonment, where he is maintained on antipsychotic medications. Whenever the daily dosage is reduced below six hundred milligrams, however, he receives a visit in his cell from Tammy.

10
SUMMARY:
THE PSYCHOTIC KILLER

T HE PSYCHOTIC KILLER is "crazy" in the lay sense. His reality is quite different from that of everyone around him. He holds strange beliefs which may eventuate in equally strange behavior. During periods when not psychotic, he may experience the world without distortion, but when in the throes of his mental derangement, he can launch an unexpected homicidal attack utterly inexplicable to those not party to his disturbed mental processes. His victim is invariably among those caught off-guard, and even the killer himself, once recovered from his acute episode, may be astonished at what he has done. Though the conduct of such individuals is to a small degree influenced by the actions and attitudes of those around them, the controlling precipitant of their homicidal act lies almost entirely within their secret, invisible, intrapsychic processes. Their victims are truly innocent and usually have no way of anticipating what is about to happen to them; short of having removed themselves physically from the lives of their killer, they could not have prevented their deaths.

Gladys's suicidal and homicidal beliefs were not rational responses to the admitted tragedy and sadness of her life. She killed because she was in a state of psychotic depression that grossly distorted her views of her sons' fortunes and future. These lethal impulses were just one part of a pervasive manic-depressive disorder continuing intermittently to this day, though presently she represents little threat to anyone, even herself. Had she not killed, she would now be in treatment as an outpatient —with occasional brief hospitalizations if her condition worsened, but her illness is one that ordinarily would allow her the freedom to live in the community. Certainly she would not be confined to a maximum-security ward peopled by custodial cases far more disabled than she, where she could sink down to the prevailing impairment rather than progressing upward to recovery. But having been found criminally insane, she is a ward of a court that requires by law that she show substantial improvement before she may be released to a more congenial and therefore more appropriate and therapeutic setting. I fear such release will never come.

Fermi, perched precariously behind his macho facade, did not become psychotic until he fell in love. Latent schizophrenics suffer a variety of mental defects, among them an inability to screen out or respond selectively to strong psychological stimuli, leaving them exquisitely vulnerable to emotional flooding; and a diffuseness of their ego boundaries—an uncertainty as to where they end and the environment begins. The fences delineating the perimeters of their psychic property are in such disrepair that what is theirs merges indistinguishably with what is others'. Their own ideas may seem to come from another; they may actually hear such thoughts as a voice from "out there." Should they fall in love, they may fuse completely with their lovers. For them, quite literally, two hearts beat as one.

Thus, Fermi experienced his lover's maturation, independence, and growing away from him not just as a loss of his woman, but as a loss of part of himself. His lethal act served only to concretize a death that for him had already occurred within his psyche. Once psychotic, he saw death as providing the only way he could reunite with his lover and thereby retrieve the stolen parts of himself.

IV

THE MASOCHISTICALLY DEPENDENT KILLER

All of us enter into romantic relationships out of a variety of near-universal needs: for intimacy, closeness, sexual gratification, a family; and out of narrower and more idiosyncratic ones, such as for status, recognition, and validation. Some people confound having these needs met with love, thinking "I love you" when what they really mean is "I must have you." For this reason they may regularly treat their lovers in many ways other than lovingly; while it would be incongrous to act hatefully toward someone for whom one felt love and affection, such behavior is not at all inconsistent vis-a-vis someone to whom one has turned largely out of narcissistic need, particularly if that person is then perceived as withholding.

When the strength of one's needs exceeds that of one's sense of self—one's "ego structure"—the needs can take control, imbuing the relationship with an addictive quality in which one becomes masochistically dependent and grasping. This powerful craving—common to those who love beyond their means—is a caricature of intimacy. It is characteristically epitomized by extreme, irrational affirmations, as, for example, "If you won't stay with me, I'll die" or "If I can't have you, then no one will."

Masochistically dependent people suffer such relationships out of the certainty that this must be their lot. They never let go because having a little is better than having none at all, and they are sure that this is the best they can do.

They daily live with the crushing pain of chronic emotional deprivation. In a few, this pain grows and metastasizes throughout their primary relationship until, for a brief moment, they may be driven beyond even their substantial limits of tolerance. At last, they put an end to their pain.

11
ON AND OFF

BY THE TIME I arrived at the jail, I already had some sense of this young couple and their consuming feelings for each other, having just spent much time reading lengthy interviews with family and friends both of Julie and of Roland—the man who killed her. Of course, though all agreed the two were deeply in love, those close to Julie did not see the relationship in the same light as those close to Roland. The question remained: Had she pursued him these last months, unable to let him go, or had he continuously pressed unwanted attentions upon her? A glance at a log of their long-distance calls had left no doubt that *neither* could go for more than a day without calling the other, right up to the time of Julie's death. Clearly, to understand this homicide would require more than a psychiatric examination of Roland —I would have to dissect the romantic bond between killer and victim, and if possible, perform a psychological autopsy of Julie as well.

Assisting me would be a psychological axiom: *Our partner in intimacy is a mirror of our inner selves.* * Irrespective of

* "The Romantic Relationship," by Carmen Lynch and Martin Blinder, in *Family Therapy*, Martin Blinder, editor; Vol. X, No. 2.

outward appearances, the person with whom we form an intimate connection reveals our *own* level of security, self-esteem, wisdom, sexual development, and integrity. Our romantic partner is our personal "portrait of Dorian Grey"—a portrait otherwise buried in the attic of our unconscious—reflecting what and where we are psychologically, whom we deserve, and what we are willing to accept.

Thus, if our partners plague us with excessive demands, it is often because *we* don't know how to set limits. If they subject us to unremitting criticism, they are merely affirming *our* own low self-esteem.

Such mutuality exists in every romantic relationship, the good and the bad in collaboration, a conspiracy between the partners' collective unconscious. Virtue never resides entirely within one nor evil entirely within the other.

Thus, a very secure person is unlikely to commit very long to someone insecure. A very independent person cannot long abide a whining, dependent one. We rarely remain intimate with individuals whose self-esteem is substantially higher or lower than our own. The longevity of our emotionally intense relationships usually depends upon our tolerance—of a significant portion of *ourselves*. Thus, there might be much of Julie in Roland —if one knew where to look.

Roland was a muscular, almost squat, sandy-haired, bespectacled man with a little-boy quality about him. He had a marked jailhouse pallor. For the greater part of the examination he was able to talk to me in a measured, coherent, even careful way, but whenever our talk moved to his relationship with Julie his controlled poise rapidly disintegrated. He became tearful, he trembled, he paced.

Anticipating this great discomfort, he had for several weeks resisted being examined. Only his attorney's insistence got him to agree to see me.

"I understand, Roland, that you're not overjoyed at the prospect of meeting with me today."

"That's right. I don't see the point of all this. I . . . I did what I did and I know what the penalty should be. I deserve whatever happens. I've ruined so many lives . . . I don't see what talking to a shrink is going to accomplish."

"I must say that it may not accomplish a thing. So if you'll just go ahead and tell me now, in a word or two, why you killed someone who—from what I've heard and read—was the most important person in your life, I'll gather up my papers and leave you in peace."

He said nothing for several minutes. Then he began to breathe faster. His eyes glistened and then filled with tears.

"I don't know . . . I don't know why I killed Julie. God! We loved each other so much . . ."

I spoke very softly. "There is some possibility, Roland, that you may not be entirely responsible for what you did . . ."

"Bullshit! *I* am entirely responsible! *Me.* I shot my most precious person to death. I should be the one who's dead."

"I promise you I am not here to challenge your views, even where I might take exception. I'm here only to try and get an understanding of what happened. Perhaps our finding out why this tragedy occurred will help with the pain."

"Maybe it will help my lawyer. Nothing will help my pain. It certainly won't help Julie."

We sat in silence for several minutes in apparent stalemate.

"I can't talk about it!"

More silence.

"I don't want to talk about it. I've nothing against you. *No* one could understand what we had—what it was like."

I nodded. "What you had was so unique that probably nobody could have enough experience or insight to enable you to get a handle on what you went through."

Silence again, then a deep sigh.

"I will never love anyone like that again. I will never find anyone for whom I will have those feelings again . . . She was a very large part of me—my heart, my soul. When she died, a large part of me died, and I can't see another woman ever bringing it back . . . Frankly, I wouldn't even want to try."

"Roland, tell me if you can—who was this Julie . . . this woman . . . this extraordinary, precious woman?"

To hear him tell it, not much of anyone—at first. Six years his junior, she was a college freshman, shy, insecure, an ungainly product of a foster home; but perhaps most important, quite taken by Roland, and quickly his devoted student.

"Julie was such a lady, quiet, a lovely little flower. She was my flower. She hadn't had much sexual experience, had never gotten off with a man, hardly ever used drugs, didn't drink at all. But as soon as we were alone, she was so . . . eager. In a week she had learned everything I knew —and went on from there."

Within a month they had fallen in love, a love marked by volcanic sexuality. It was the first really close relationship for either of them, and each almost swallowed up the other: Because of the other, each became transformed from *nobody* to *somebody*.

As he spoke of Julie, Roland's demeanor changed. He became animated, seemed actually to get larger before my eyes, and his face began to glow.

"Wherever we went, people always asked us who we were—were we movie stars or something? They'd wonder about us, ask questions, send us drinks, invite themselves to our table. Julie was always hanging on my arm. We were always kissing. People would think we were on our honeymoon. We were special people. Because of Julie my entire life was different. It was like, for the first time, night had ended and I could see daylight."

Certainly, it had been a dark, difficult twenty-four years till then, beginning, inevitably, with the quality of the parenting Roland had received.

"I see now that I was never really happy, never really a person until I met Julie. I felt different from my friends —not that I actually had any when I was still at home. It was just that my parents are different than other parents. I don't remember them ever coming right out and telling me that they loved me. We don't ever have little chats. We don't talk about things that are bothering me, or my future, or even the weather. The only time my father communicates with me at all is when he's lecturing or shouting at me about something."

As a child, Roland perceived his father, a prosperous electrical contractor, as "big, powerful, self-assured— someone to look up to." During his teenage years, father and son enjoyed target practice, hunting and fishing together; his father was also quite supportive of Roland's athletic activities and prowess. But when Roland turned sixteen and wanted reduced parental supervision, the right to lock his room and go out in the evening without detailed explanations, his father "turned into a cop. He really began leaning on me."

Roland did not understand this—hadn't he always been a well-behaved and obedient boy? Why this pressure all of a sudden? He wanted to but could not talk to his father about it. "My father always lived behind a stone wall."

"And your mother?"

"She was usually wherever my father was. Sort of like his echo. She went to church every week and did what everybody else thought was right. She would get on my case, but not as much as he did. Anything he said or did, she would go along with."

Surprisingly, that included the heavy use of alcohol.

"Both my parents drank a lot. Both of them could really hold it. My whole family—Mom, Dad, my brothers, my three sisters—all of us take to drinking. But my father drinks day and night. I've seen him down half a gallon of vodka without showing it."

"That sort of drinking impresses you about your father?"

Roland nodded. "He taught me how to drink and be cool about it—I might hardly be able to crawl home but you'd never know it."

Upon graduating high school, Roland attended the University of Idaho for a year. He admitted that he was much more absorbed by skiing, fraternity life, and the feeling of freedom than he was by the demands of scholarship. He barely passed his freshman finals and the following year settled for a junior college near his home in Syracuse; soon he left and worked awhile for his father as a warehouseman, then went through a series of relatively short-term jobs.

He states that his father became increasingly impatient with him at this point; or rather, however much Roland tried or even succeeded, his father would raise his expectations proportionately. Roland asked repeatedly to be given the opportunity to follow in his father's footsteps, to learn the family business and hold a responsible position there. His father replied that he wasn't ready, "wasn't settled enough." The only tasks he found for him were menial and subordinate. Roland, in turn, "just went through the motions."

"So one day my father cut me loose. He said I wasn't living life according to the rules. He told me I was on my own."

Roland, now age twenty-three, moved to an apartment and "hung out," living on unemployment supplemented by a few odd jobs. He was drinking quite heavily—in fact by this time he had accumulated four drunk-driving arrests for which he served several months in county jail.

Shortly thereafter he states that he "saw the light" and decided to return to "real schooling," enrolling at the University of Syracuse—his father's alma mater. He concentrated more on his studies and also joined the intercollegiate boxing team, which helped him to put aside the heavy drinking. Things even improved perceptibly with his father toward the end of the year when word got back home of his accomplishments as a boxer. But what was most important about Syracuse was that it was there that he met Julie.

Things progressed rapidly. By the summer of 1978 they were living together; in January of 1979, over the objections of Julie's foster parents, they became engaged and committed to a marriage date of August 1. The week following their decision, Roland's father gave his son the job he had been waiting for all of his young life—that of plant superintendent.

"I guess my father had just been waiting for me to really settle down. And thanks to Julie, I had. The job won me respect. For the first time I really felt that I was my father's son. I was in line to be successful and wealthy."

He had also won new status in the eyes of the blue-collar workers in his father's company who had made fun of him when, in those first years, his father had assigned him to the dirtiest, most demeaning jobs. "Now I could work in 'real clothes'—not some scruffy uniform. And I was certain that someday I would be running that company."

Meanwhile, his relationship with Julie had become even more heated. "It seemed like she had me spellbound. She controlled me. Nothing like this had ever happened to me before, like I couldn't get out of bed and tie my shoes until I talked to her. It was scary how much I needed her."

It appeared to him—perhaps retrospectively—that Julie seemed to get some special gratification from his emotional weakness, his growing dependence upon her. When he was feeling insecure she would become haughty and self-confident, but when he pulled himself together, *she* would become manifestly dependent and would move toward him lovingly again. They were in many ways mirror images of the other.

Both Julie and Roland were alternately euphoric in

their sense of oneness and frightened by what was happening to them. Each seemed to have an intense narcissistic need for the other, a product of their early deprivation, a form of psychopathology bonding them together. Nevertheless, it was, as Roland put it, "the best year of my life in every way—in all ways."

Then, beginning about June, Julie seemed to withdraw. Though clearly still devoted to Roland, she was having increasing difficulty facing the idea of a permanent commitment to him. Additionally, her foster parents' opposition to her marrying—particularly marrying Roland—failed to soften with time. In their view, she was too young and Roland was the wrong husband for her at any age.

On the Fourth of July they had a big fight, during which Julie admitted that she was dating another man. That ended their engagement, but they continued to see each other and maintain a sexual relationship, though Julie soon became involved with several others as well. Purportedly she told Roland that she would always love him but was simply not ready to settle down with one man.

Roland then received another blow. "When we broke our engagement my father turned his back on me. For awhile there it had seemed to me like I truly had a father, that we were friends like we had been when I was a kid . . . he even put his arm around me once. My mother was really happy with me. But after Julie left, my father and I never talked anymore. Julie held the key to everything, not just to our relationship but to my family, my future, my life."

The next eight months, Roland and Julie shared an

intense on-again-off-again relationship, "dating," fighting, breaking up and then reconciling. As Roland explained it, any hint that he was seeing other women would bring Julie back to him; she seemed to need the security of their relationship plus the freedom to see others. Their fights grew increasingly acrimonious, on one occasion culminating in Roland apparently getting Julie into what he called a "headlock," which put her in a neck brace for two weeks.

This was the final straw for Julie's foster father, who insisted she transfer to the University of Rochester. Roland resigned himself at last to the end of their relationship and began putting together a life that did not revolve around Julie.

But even the two hundred miles that had been placed between them helped little, for almost immediately, Julie started phoning Roland, telling him that she did not wish to lose him. She might come home from a date at two in the morning and call him, all soft, loving, and appealing, and talk to him about their getting married, about how she was unhappy in Rochester and how they should go "straight to Reno." Periodically, her loving mode lasted long enough for them to spend a weekend together. On one such occasion, she showed him a special dress she had bought for their wedding day.

"She even put it on and danced around in it. God! She was beautiful. But then I couldn't reach her at all for the next ten days. She was out every night, and once when I did happen to catch her in, she couldn't talk."

Of course, Roland was now thoroughly hooked again and utterly bewildered. He would spend hours sitting in his room, talking to his tape recorder for company. He slept all day and wandered about at night. He flirted briefly with the idea of suicide. He was drinking ever more heroic quantities of alcohol.

"I was utterly confused, Doctor. She bounced me backwards and forwards between commitment and no relationship at all. One day I would experience intense pain—worse than the worst physical pain I've ever known. Then she'd tell me how much she missed me, wanted to have my children, and I'd go higher than a kite. It sounded real, so real. But she'd sounded real many times before—then broken away and run to other men. So when she reached out to me, some days I'd go for it. Other days I'd get mad. I'd feel manipulated and close her off. Then, maybe two days later, I'd be on the phone begging her to see me."

The last week of Julie's life was a compressed recapitulation of all the conflicts of the previous six months. On Monday she phoned and told Roland that he was the only man in the world for her—that she had to see him tomorrow. On Tuesday, just as he was about to leave the house, she called to tell him that it would never work; they must not see each other again. On Wednesday she called to say that she could not live without him. On Thursday he called her only to learn that it was all over. On Friday she called to tell him that he was the only possible person she could marry, that he had to come to her at once.

Roland could not wait for Saturday's call. Bearing his father's revolver and a very high blood-alcohol level, he got into his car at dawn and drove up to Rochester and to the women's dormitory complex. Arriving at the university at about eight-thirty A.M., he stopped at a gas station and called Julie. No answer. He then drove past her building, saw her car parked out front, found another phone, and called again. Still no answer.

"By now I was feeling foolish. I didn't know what to do. I wasn't even sure why I was there in the first place. I decided to go home. I got back in the car and drove past Julie's place one more time. Then I spotted her. She was walking with this guy along the path from the student center down the block. I got out of the car and ran down the street to meet her. God—it was good to see her face.

"She said, 'Oh, Roland,' but then turned away! She told this guy she'd see him later and just walked toward her apartment. I was smiling, reaching out for her, and *she turned away!* I called after her. I told her I wanted to talk to her. She said she couldn't talk to me now and went inside. I remember thinking, 'Julie, why are you blowing it for us?'

"I knocked on the door. She didn't answer, so I started to go in. The door was stuck . . ."

"Stuck or locked?"

"Just stuck. I pushed hard and it jerked open. My gun fell out of my waistband, right there in the doorway. I started to pick it up . . . then I saw Julie. Our eyes met and she started to back away from me, shaking her head. I pulled the trigger twice . . . I don't know why . . . she fell backwards. I ran out the door, got into my car, and got the hell out of there. They stopped me on the Thruway about a half-hour later . . . for drunk driving."

Roland was now slumped in his chair, exhausted. It was clear to me that whatever psychiatric conclusions I might draw, and whatever the trial outcome, he was going to need a great deal of emotional support and psychotherapy. After I finished my examination, I encouraged him to accept visits from the jail's mental-health worker and told him that I would make arrangements for them. He agreed.

Two months later, however, when at eight in the morning on the first day of Roland's trial, the bailiff went to his cell to collect and transport him to the courthouse, he found him dead, hanging by his belt from a hook in the ceiling.

12

TO LOVE, HONOR, AND OBEY

"THE DEFENSE may call and swear in her next witness. The defense calls Dr. Martin Blinder . . . Dr. Blinder, you've testified as a psychiatric expert in court before?"

"Yes, I have."

"Would you be so kind as to summarize for the jury your qualifications as a psychiatrist."

"The prosecution will stipulate as to the doctor's qualifications."

"Very well. Doctor, you examined my client—Lisa Williams—did you not?"

"Yes, I examined her on May 5 and 19 in my office in San Francisco."

"What was the purpose of that examination?"

"To determine her state of mind on February 12 of this year, the date she fatally shot her husband, and to gain some understanding of the reasons for her offense."

"At whose request did you perform this examination?"

"I was one of two psychiatrists appointed by the court."

"Do you perform this sort of psychiatric examination with some frequency?"

"Yes, I do."

"How does this usually come about?"

"Typically, the court will have some questions that can only be resolved after it receives information about a defendant's state of mind, so it will appoint me to make the appropriate inquiry. At other times, a defense attorney such as yourself may ask me to examine her client, or the prosecution may request such an examination."

"Doctor, can you explain to the jury, please, what the typical psychiatric examination for these purposes consists of?"

"Certainly. It's pretty standard. First, I take a past history of the defendant to learn all that I can—within the time constraints—about who he is, how he got that way, the critical life experiences that enabled him to become the kind of person he is. We then focus on the circumstances around his offense, his perceptions of what led up to it, and the offense itself. Finally—although this occurs throughout the history-taking—I perform a mental-status examination. Here I focus on relatively objective measures of how the defendant's mind is actually functioning in the moment—the quality of his thought processes, emotional state, perceptual apparatus, behavior, and so on. All this together allows me to establish the diagnosis."

"What do you mean by 'diagnosis'—do psychiatrists make a diagnosis just like doctors do?"

"In all due respect, Counsel, I *am* a doctor—an M.D. —went to medical school, had an internship, residency, delivered my share of babies, and all that. I don't think you'd want to entrust your appendix to me at this point, but I'm still licensed in the State of California to remove it."

"I stand corrected, Doctor. Please explain, then, how do you make a psychiatric diagnosis?"

"Just as in other branches of medicine, the psychiatrist gathers up symptoms and signs and then connects them, like dots on a page. The image—the clinical pattern—that emerges is the diagnosis.

"A cardiologist might obtain a history from a fifty-three-year-old obese chain-smoker who has symptoms of sudden crushing substernal chest pain radiating down the left arm, shortness of breath, and a family history of premature death due to high blood pressure; he connects these 'dots' and the picture that then emerges is that of a heart attack. Similarly, a psychiatrist might obtain a history from a seventeen-year-old overachiever just starting college, of recent social apprehension and withdrawal, followed by obsessive paranoid thoughts and the hearing of voices; most psychiatrists would discern the clinical pattern of schizophrenia."

"So then a psychiatrist diagnoses and treats mental disorders much in the same way other doctors treat physical disorders?"

"Your Honor, I object to the defense counsel leading her witness."

"Overruled. Dr. Blinder has testified here many times before and I doubt very much if any lawyer is going to lead him someplace where he does not wish to go. Please continue, Counsel."

"Thank you, Your Honor. Now, Doctor, let me ask you —what kind of patients do you treat?"

"My practice is limited to people who have some emotional problem—though certainly not always a formal mental disorder such as schizophrenia or depression. There may be an intractable marital conflict, or perhaps excessive affection for certain seductive chemicals, or, say, difficulty with a child who, though bright, spends most of his class time cutting up. I see very ordinary kinds of people—carpenters, schoolteachers, businessmen, housewives. Over the years I have had several psychiatrists in treatment. And quite a few lawyers."

"Well, it's good to know that I have some place to go if I have to."

"Any judges, Dr. Blinder?"

"Not at present, Your Honor."

"It's always gratifying to hear an affirmation as to the stability of the judiciary from so reputable a source. Please continue with your witness, Counsel."

"Thank you, Your Honor."

"Now, Doctor, when you examined Lisa Williams, were you able to reach a diagnosis as to her probable mental state at or about at two A.M., February 12?"

"I believe so."

"And that diagnosis?"

"I diagnosed Mrs. Williams as suffering a severe depressive reaction. Further, she has long had an underlying passive-dependent personality disorder with marked masochistic traits."

"That's quite a mouthful, Doctor. I think I'm going to have to ask you to explain each one of those words, one by one, to the jury, but first: Can you tell us how you arrived at that diagnosis?"

"Through that process I described earlier—the history and mental-status examination."

"All right, what history did you obtain from Mrs. Williams?"

"I learned that she was twenty-four years old at the time of her husband's death, born and raised in Modesto, California, living almost her entire life within the same few streets. She describes her parents as extremely hard-working, proper, church-going, stern but well-meaning middle-class people, who early on impressed upon their only daughter the value of propriety, neatness, and prompt discharge of responsibilities and payment of bills. No smoking, drinking, or open expression of feelings were permitted in her family.

"Mrs. Williams worked diligently to meet her parents' standards. She sang in the church choir, allowed herself no bad habits, suppressed any feelings of anger she might ever have had, and in fact did all she could to keep spankings to a minimum.

"In addition to its uncommon strictness, her childhood was marked by a series of five eye operations, beginning at eighteen months, which were quite frightening to her; by a constant 'nervousness' for which she received counseling intermittently through adolescence; and by a 'weak bladder' for whose inopportune discharge she was frequently punished and humiliated. She also remembers her fellow students making fun of what she called her 'Benjamin Franklin eyeglasses,' which she had to wear following eye operations. These glasses were literally taped to her head to ensure that they would stay in the proper position.

"As a child she frequently had the feeling her peers 'picked on' her, but things improved in high school and junior college, where she made a few close friends and obtained acceptable grades."

"It doesn't sound as if Mrs. Williams had a terrifically happy childhood, does it?"

"No—it certainly doesn't."

"What is the significance of this, Doctor? You know, lots of folk have miserable childhoods. You're not going to suggest that this is why Mrs. Williams shot her husband?"

"No, of course not. Its relevance lies in the contribution it made to the type of grownup Mrs. Williams became—to her adult personality. And I think it starts to explain why she was unusually susceptible to the stresses she experienced in her marriage, why she had the kind of marriage she did, and why it ended so tragically."

"Well, Doctor, perhaps you had better tell us about Mrs. Williams's marriage."

"Okay. But first let me state that as an adolescent, she did some dating but had no serious romances—and certainly no sexual experiences—until meeting her future husband, Roger, in 1959. They became engaged in December of 1960. She actually spent relatively little time with him throughout their two-and-a-half-year courtship because of Roger's military obligation, which he discharged overseas. Neither did they have intercourse until the wedding night, Mrs. Williams firmly believing in 'saving sex for the wedding bells,' if I may use her quaint phrase.

"Though Mrs. Williams still maintains that there were many moments of joy, my gentle but persistent questioning revealed that marriage proved from the very beginning to offer little but deprivation and abuse. Her marriage, which she had anticipated would be much like that of her parents, in fact turned out to be quite different."

"How so, Doctor?"

"Within a few days of the wedding, Roger revealed himself to be an immature, irresponsible, rather violent young man. Sporadically employed, he spent most of what little money he made on himself; his wife, and soon their child, frequently went without food. He even used the welfare checks the family received when he was out of work for a time to finance gambling sprees. He would often strike his wife and seemed to derive some perverse satisfaction from seeing her cry. He was inconsiderate in meeting his sexual appetites—the only use Mrs. Williams felt he had for her. He would sometimes be gone for thirty-six hours without a word of notice or explanation to her, and yet was subject to emotional explosions should he return and not find *her* at home. He regularly lied to her. When walking with her in public, he would alternately ignore her by making her walk ten feet behind him, or humiliate her by walking just beside her while he covered her crotch with his hand."

"Why did she put up with this, Doctor?"

"She loved him, she didn't know any better, and she didn't know what else to do. She tells me that she swore to 'love, honor, and obey' and she was bound to stick to that."

"All right, please continue, Doctor."

"Roger would make outlandish accusations. Mrs. Williams reports that he was something of a racist. Periodically he accused her of having intercourse with various Mexican men from the neighborhood. He claimed that their daughter was not his child. She states he pushed her down the stairs several times when she was pregnant in an attempt to induce a miscarriage."

"Have you documentation of this?"

"Only the hospital records, which indicate three 'accidental falls' down a flight of stairs within one week, during her first few months of pregnancy. The records indi-

cate that these falls followed immediately upon—I believe they say—'a quarrel with her husband.' "

"Doctor, I invite your attention to these papers—are
these the hospital records to which you refer?"

"Yes."

"Your Honor, I should like to have these records entered into evidence as Defense Exhibit 5."

"Any prosecution objections?"

"None, Your Honor."

"The records are admitted. Continue, please, Counsel."

"Anything else, Doctor, you deemed significant about
Mrs. Williams's marriage?"

"Yes. On one occasion, Roger apparently broke all of
the dining-room windows and then turned upon her with
his fists. She states that he continuously made her feel—
as she said—'ugly and repulsive.' He thought tenderness
of any sort effeminate and conducted himself accordingly. Mrs. Williams reports that she felt 'trapped in a
hostile house to do his work.' Roger degraded her and
treated her sadistically, but she felt there was nothing she
could do but suffer.

"I should tell you that all this is an illustrative, rather
than an exhaustive, description of Roger's difficulties
with the role of husband and father, as perceived by his
wife but confirmed by others."

"Doctor, you read transcripts of testimony given by
friends and relatives of the Williams' in this court last
week, did you not?"

"Yes."

"Was what you read consistent with the history you
yourself obtained from Mrs. Williams?"

"Yes."

"All right. How long did this abuse go on, Doctor?"

"They were married for four years. Most of those four years were pretty bad."

"What was Mrs. Williams's reaction to all this?"

"It was not entirely atypical—not at all unusual in my experience. Rather than cause her to leave her husband, his indifference and brutality seemed only to make her struggle all the more to 'keep up her part' and 'save the marriage.' She begged and cajoled him to change, to give her love and show that he cared about the marriage. She pleaded with him to join her in marriage counseling, all without success.

"She started to develop psychosomatic symptoms, such as palpitations and feelings of suffocation. She had suicidal obsessions, though the actual act was inhibited by thoughts of what would happen to her child were she gone. She felt oppressed by her husband's presence, but despondent and lonely in his absence. She lost weight, was chronically hungry yet paradoxically repelled by food. Occasionally she would find herself screaming, breaking things, and shouting obscenities without really knowing their meaning.

"It is significant that, a few years previously, already desperate for some sort of affection, she had turned to a seventeen-year-old delivery boy and had had a brief affair with him. She confessed her transgression at once to her husband in the hope that it would force some changes. Roger accepted her admission with seeming indifference at the time, but later delighted in throwing it back at her. I suspect that this affair, so utterly out of character for Mrs. Williams, heralded the beginning of the illness responsible for the tragedy that followed."

"Doctor, would you be so kind as to describe to the

ladies and gentleman of the jury the nature and evolution of that illness.''

"In the weeks preceding the homicide, the marriage virtually fell apart. Roger was spending less and less time at home, gave his wife less and less money for food, ignored their child, and was indifferent to her pleas. He seemed even to lose interest in her sexually.

"She received word that Stewart, the adolescent to whom she had once turned for solace, had summarily married. She began having night terrors—illusions, while in semi-sleep, of being attacked. She felt tired much of the time and yet unable to sleep.

"About two weeks before the shooting, Mrs. Williams stated that Roger, in a rage over something, placed the tip of a knife against her trachea and screamed obscenities at her. A few days later, he conspicuously dug his rifle out of a closet, pointed it at her, and dramatically debated out loud with himself as to whether or not he should pull the trigger.''

"When was this?"

"This was early in February.''

"Please continue, Doctor.''

"Well, I guess this brings the history pretty much up to date. February 11th, the night prior to the shooting, Mrs. Williams reports that she was alone as usual, and feeling physically and emotionally exhausted. She describes herself as 'feeling strange,' as if all of her were not quite together. It was hard for her to think. The only thought she can remember now is an idea going around and around that Roger was her husband in name only— that she really didn't have a marriage.

"She was unusually tense, tremulous, and weepy, feelings that were perhaps exacerbated by the imminence of menses. What little food there was she had given to their daughter, and her hunger added to her sense of insecurity and spiritual emptiness. Exhausted—she had been up since six A.M.—yet unable to sleep, she dashed about the house with a sort of nervous energy.

"Roger was long overdue at home. She felt—in her words—'terribly alone' and 'lost,' experienced a 'tremendous longing' for him and a desperate need—and I quote—'to make him realize how serious everything was and how much his family needed his attention.'

"She began to worry that he had been hurt or killed, and started phoning around for him. She finally located him at the home of friends, where he was playing cards. She pleaded with him to come home. He promised to return shortly, but by four A.M., still hadn't come in. She called but was told by his friend to 'quit pestering them,' and that he would be along in a few minutes.

"At five-thirty A.M., he still hadn't arrived. Should she call the police? The hospital? Where was he? Why was he doing this to her?

"Without sleep for almost twenty-four hours now, nearly hysterical, and unable to reason clearly, she tried to think of some dramatic gesture to get through to her husband how distressed she felt and how much she needed him to *do* something—to come back to her—to save their marriage. She went to the closet and took out his rifle. With *this* she could underline her anguish and convey to Roger—clearly and unmistakably—the sense of loss she felt within her. She wished not to alienate or injure him but to rouse him to greater effort.

"She heard him come up the walk. Her arms, cradling the rifle, felt very heavy. As the door opened, she pointed the rifle *above* the doorway, shut her eyes, and squeezed the trigger. It was the first time in her life that she had ever used a firearm.

"However, when she fired, the gun, 'as if possessed by demons,' as she put it—but more likely powered by hostility of which she was consciously unaware—moved to point directly at Roger. A shot rang out and he fell backwards.

"Immediately she ran over to him, not wanting to believe that she had hurt him. Earlier in their marriage he had frequently feigned death, as a little joke. But this time Roger was not joking. The sudden realization of what she had done hit her. She screamed, 'My God, I've shot him, I've shot him!' "

"Your Honor, if the court please, I think this would be a good time to take our noon recess."

"Very well. Ladies and gentlemen of the jury, you are not to discuss this case among yourselves or with anyone else. Please be back at one-thirty. This court is recessed."

"Now, Doctor, before we broke for lunch you summarized the history of the homicide you obtained from Mrs. Williams. What did you do next?"

"I then performed a mental-status examination of the defendant."

"And what did this reveal?"

"It revealed Mrs. Williams to be a shy, demure, pleasant, extremely well-groomed, controlled young woman. She dressed simply and wore little makeup. She was quite inhibited and her speech spotlessly cleansed of suggestive or profane words. There was a naive honesty in her manner. She gave her account of the shooting with an air of disbelief, suggesting that she had not yet fully assimilated the fact of her husband's death or her role in it. Her memory for the mechanics of the fatal night was good, having progressively improved since an amnesia immediately following the shooting, although she was at a loss to account for how she, as she stated, 'could ever have done such a terrible thing.'

"During the course of the examination, it was clear that she identified with children and with small, helpless animals. She told me how they are 'so easily hurt and can't talk back.' She described how she was overwhelmed in the recent past by the loss of her pet cat and dog. She cried when touching on her own lethal actions.

"She was in all respects appropriate, rational, coherent, and free from delusions, hallucinations, and other stigmata of psychosis, though still imbued with a rather primitive religiosity. She believed herself to have been momentarily 'possessed by demons' the night of the killing—demons which, in a sense, have been exorcised through her husband's death.

"She gave her narrative in somewhat obsessive detail, and was clearly torn between accurately describing her husband's failings on the one hand, and her dependent longing for him on the other. Strong feelings rippled below the surface as she told how he had treated her. Yet it was clearly difficult for her to say anything bad about him. She wished with some intensity that he were alive to hold her in his arms—to care for her. The prospect of being a widow was terrifying. She was almost entirely unaware of any hostile feelings she might have felt and probably still feels toward him, and was conscious only of a keen desire for him to be alive today, though perhaps as a different man than the one he was."

"Thank you, Doctor. Now I assume you put all of this together—'connected the dots' is how I think you stated it—and arrived at a diagnosis. You gave it to us this morning. Would you be so kind as to explain to the jury what those terms mean?"

"Surely. First, I believe Mrs. Williams was suffering from a profound depression."

"Let me interrupt you for a moment here. You know, Doctor, I must tell you that from time to time my husband gets depressed. He goes out to do some errands and the car doesn't start, then it begins to rain and that leak in the roof we supposedly had fixed just last week isn't fixed after all, and I'm supposed to meet him at six o'clock for dinner but don't show up until nine-thirty, and by that time he is really *depressed* and says a few pointed things to me, and then *I* get depressed. Is that what you mean?"

"No, not at all. When psychiatrists use the word 'depression,' we use it with a capital D, referring not just to social discomfort but to a true mental disorder with definite signs and symptoms, and a likelihood of response to specific treatments. It is a serious condition. A few patients with this disorder, if left untreated, will go on to take their own lives."

"And Mrs. Williams had this condition on the morning she shot her husband?"

"At the moment she shot her husband, and for many weeks—perhaps months—prior to that."

"Would you explain the other components of your diagnosis?"

"I stated that she had a lifelong passive-dependent personality disorder with masochistic traits, by which I mean that all of her life she has been dependent upon others for approval and for self-esteem. She thinks so poorly of herself that she almost considers it her 'due' to be punished. It hurts and she doesn't like it, but she has been brought up to believe that that's the way it's going to be. Unconsciously she seeks it out. She has never known any other kind of life. She went from criticism by her parents to criticism by her peers to criticism by her husband. She has never known how to say 'This is ridiculous. I don't deserve this. I *won't* put up with it.' She has been well brought up to put up with it—until finally, because of the intensity of misery and her depression, she could put up with it no longer."

"Doctor, do you believe Mrs. Williams wanted her husband dead?"

"No. I believe she loved her husband—loves him still. She wishes he were here—alive. Different, perhaps, but alive."

"Could she premediate or form malice?"

"I can't answer that very well—those are legal questions requiring a legal answer from the jury. I would think the psychiatric data that I have presented would play a part in that answer, but only a part."

"And that part?"

"The clinical data I have obtained indicates that the mental functions necessary for premeditation and the forming of malice were significantly compromised by her emotional condition—her mental disorder. I cannot tell you how *much* they were affected—I think you will have to draw your own conclusions—but certainly, they would have had to have been affected to a measurable extent."

"Was she insane?"

"That, too, is a legal question that I must leave to the jury. I can say that, yes, certainly, she had some awareness that she was firing a rifle and that ordinarily she would know that it was wrong to fire a lethal weapon at another human being. But at the time she shot her husband, she did not have very good access to this information and was not in very good shape to apply it. Whether or not she was actually legally insane would depend upon the weight you give these factors, and to a lot of other evidence that has already been presented or will be presented later, to which I am not privy."

"Well, Doctor, perhaps you can answer this—did this young woman intend to kill her husband?"

"I think she intended to *change* him."

"Doctor, were it not for Mrs. Williams's mental illness, do you think Roger would be dead this day?"

"No, I do not."

"Thank you, Doctor. No further questions. Your witness."

"Prosecution, you may cross-examine."

"Thank you, Your Honor."

"Hello, Doctor Blinder. As you know, I am Robert Elias, Deputy District Attorney, representing the People of California in this matter. Doctor, Mrs. Williams has never been your patient, has she—you've never actually treated her, have you?"

"No. I simply performed a diagnostic evaluation."

"How much time did you spend with her altogether?"

"About four hours."

"Do you really think you can find out all the important things about a person's psyche in just four hours?"

"No. But I think I am able to find out enough to offer competent testimony about a fairly limited, circumscribed area of an individual's life—in this case, Mrs. Williams's criminal act, her state of mind during one particular time in her life."

"How much time do you spend with an individual you have in treatment—it's many weeks, isn't it?"

"Yes."

"Months?"

"Yes. Sometimes even years."

"You need all that time?"

"Yes, often."

"Compared to years, four hours doesn't seem very long."

"No, I suppose not. But you must remember that many of those years are devoted to treatment. Most doctors—in any specialty, really—will make a diagnosis the very first time you see them. Sometimes in twenty minutes. Then they treat. You don't usually keep coming back to the doctor over and over again, just for a diagnosis. You expect him to make it on the first shot, give you some medicine, begin treatment, and send you on your way. Psychiatry is no different, although admittedly, treatment will often go on for a much longer period of time. It can be lifelong, just as the treatment of the diabetic can be lifelong. But the diagnosis can generally be made fairly quickly."

"But in those cases where you have more extended contact with the patient, you will often change your diagnosis with more information, won't you?"

"Yes, that can happen."

"So that if you had spent more time with Mrs. Williams, you might have had cause to offer some opinions very different from those you gave us today."

"I don't think so. But it's possible."

"Doctor, how do you know whether or not your diagnosis today is correct?"

"How do I know? I'm not certain I can ever really *know*,

in an absolute sense—there's no psychiatric platinum bar in Washington against which I may measure my judgment."

"In fact, Doctor, another psychiatrist examining Mrs. Williams might come up with conclusions quite different from yours?"

"Yes. But most likely, those differences would be ones of terminology, not of substance. Or, if a psychiatrist is encouraged to go outside his clinical data and offer a legal opinion, yes, then you do sometimes get some diametrically opposed views. But in my long experience as a forensic psychiatrist, even several psychiatrists examining the same patient will see him or her in much the same way, recording the same symptoms and usually reaching the same basic diagnosis. It would be hard for me to imagine in this case, for example, any psychiatrist or psychologist finding Mrs. Williams anything but suffering from some form of depression prior to the homicide, plus a lifelong personality disorder with much passivity, dependency, and masochism. As to the *legal significance* of those clinical observations . . . well, that's another matter."

"Doctor, psychiatrists *do* have clinical disagreements, do they not?"

"Yes."

"In fact, you are familiar, are you not, with the work of psychiatrist Dr. Thomas Szasz which proves that there is no such thing as mental illness."

"His writings express his *opinion.* They are not *proof* of anything. I've often wondered what the good doctor does for the anguished individuals who presumably come to him for treatment for a constellation of symptoms any first-year psychiatric resident would recognize as, say, the manic-depressive syndrome, or perhaps, schizophrenia. If you recognize these conditions, you can treat them quite effectively. But I have no idea what Dr. Szasz does in such a situation. Does he tell them their mental illness, their suffering, is a myth and send them away? What might he offer the stewardess who escapes a plane crash uninjured but is left so anxious and fearful that she cannot even go down to the airport to pick up her last paycheck? Does he accuse her of making it all up —of having no backbone? If these mental illnesses are not real, then how does he account for a particular medication being so consistently effective for condition A but not condition B, whereas the reverse is consistently true when the drug is chosen from a different chemical group?"

"Well, let us leave Dr. Szasz, then, sir, since the two of you seem to agree on so little, and go back to you and Mrs. Williams. Doctor, I believe this morning you testified that the defendant was in all respects appropriate, rational, coherent, and free from delusions, hallucinations, and other stigmata of psychosis. That's an accurate quote of what you said, isn't it, Doctor?"

"Yes."

"In other words, Doctor, there is no evidence that this woman is, or was ever, psychotic?"

"None."

" 'Psychosis' is a word psychiatrists use to describe someone that the lay person would see as crazy."

"Yes."

"In other words, Mrs. Williams is not crazy."

"No . . . she is not."

"She knows what's going on?"

"Yes."

"Very much the sort of person responsible for her actions?"

"Generally, yes."

"Doctor, you testified this morning that the defendant committed adultery—there was nothing psychotic about that?"

"No . . . ill-advised, but not psychotic. I do think, however . . ."

"Thank you, Doctor. You have answered my question."

"Objection, Your Honor. I think the doctor should be allowed to complete his answer."

"Yes. Mr. Elias, please allow the witness to finish his answer. Doctor, did you wish to add something?"

"Yes, Your Honor . . . merely that I think this adulterous act was very much out of character for Mrs. Williams and was performed less out of . . . pleasure or lust . . . than out of despair. This change in her was a part of the very mental disorder that ultimately culminated in her committing homicide. It's true, I certainly do not think she ever was psychotic, but neither was she in good emotional shape at that time either."

"Doctor, there are many different schools of psychiatry, aren't there?"

"Historically, yes. But today, these different streams of thought have coalesced into one large mainstream—a river, if you will—of modern psychiatry. And those differences that persist apply more to treatment philosophy than to diagnosis."

"Well, which school do you believe in *most*, Doctor? Do you believe in Freud, Jung, or Skinner . . .?"

"That's like asking me if I believe in penicillin or tetracycline. The three gentlemen you mentioned and dozens of others have all made contributions in the first half of this century to what we know about the workings of the human mind. I have learned what I could from them. They certainly had their sectarian fights, but most of them are long gone now. Their discoveries remain and continue to prove useful."

"So you just borrow a little from here, a little from there?"

"I object. Argumentative."

"I believe, Counsel, we can allow the prosecutor some latitude. This is cross-examination. Objection is over-ruled. You may answer the question, Doctor."

"Yes, Your Honor . . . I believe most psychiatrists today are fairly eclectic and bring to bear whatever tools they have. But I must admit, I *do* have a therapeutic bias. I have been trained extensively in family therapy, and when performing treatment, prefer to see my patients in the context of their families whenever possible."

"But you never treated Mrs. Williams or her family, did you?"

"No, I did not."

"You never laid eyes on the man she killed, did you?"

"No, I did not."

"In fact, most of what you know, or think you know, about Roger Williams you learned from Lisa Williams."

"That's true."

"Hardly an objective observer?"

"That's true. But one of the virtues of doing a lot of family and marital-couple work, is that you can often detect familial patterns even when you have only one-half of the system to work with. If you give me half of a photograph of an igloo, or of a Victorian house, I've got a pretty good idea what the other half of the photo is going to look like."

"You would be a lot more confident, though, Doctor, if you had personally examined *Mr.* Williams?"

"Certainly. However, I did not come here to diagnose *Mr.* Williams. I offer only Mrs. Williams's perceptions of him. But then, *her* perceptions of him were what determined the nature of her mental disorder. And it is *her* mental disorder that I perceive as the issue—at least as far as my testimony is concerned."

"But you would have preferred to examine Mr. Williams, too, before opining as to the true nature of their relationship?"

"Yes."

"But by the time you entered the case, Mr. Williams was no longer susceptible to a psychiatric examination?"

"Objection!"

"I'll withdraw the question. Doctor, isn't it a fact that most of your conclusions depend upon what the defendant told you, and if much of what she told you is not true, then your conclusions would not be worth a great deal?"

"Yes, assuming that I failed to recognize her untruthfulness."

"You will allow, Doctor, that individuals you examine after they have committed a criminal charge are different than people that you examine for purposes of treatment—that someone you're examining for the court has a much greater incentive to mislead you than someone who comes to you because they want your help in treatment."

"Yes. But if I may add, I do a great number of these court examinations. After a while you get pretty good at detecting when individuals are lying to you or at least attempting to push the examination in a certain direction. It's just like the patrolman on the beat. At three in the morning he sees someone standing in a doorway jiggling the doorknob and asks the guy what he is doing and the guy says, 'Nuthin.' After a few years, the patrolman is pretty good at knowing when 'nuthin' indeed means 'nuthin,' and when it means 'something.' In fact, his life may depend upon it. So it is with forensic psychiatry. After a while, you get pretty good at distinguishing truth-tellers from liars."

"But you're not infallible, are you, Doctor?"

"Certainly not."

"In fact, if Mrs. Williams had succeeded in fooling you, then by definition you would believe her to be honest."

"Of course that's true. I wish only to point out that it is harder to fool me than you might think. One spots internal inconsistencies. The verbal and nonverbal messages don't match. There is no recognizable clinical pattern, the malingerer borrowing one symptom from here, another from there. Being schizophrenic, say, is a lot different from acting crazy."

"Now, Doctor, you stated that you did a *forensic* psychiatric examination of Mrs. Williams. Just what is *forensic* psychiatry?"

"That's a subspeciality of psychiatry concerned with the relationship between psychiatry and law, predicated upon the happy assumption that there *is* a relationship."

"It has nothing to do with treatment?"

"No."

"It means you go to court a lot?"

"No, it means I go to court occasionally. It means that I am *willing* to go to court. Most of the time, thank heavens, I simply have to write a report."

"But you are willing to go to court?"

"Certainly."

"Doctor, how much are you being paid for your testimony?"

"I'm not being paid anything."

"What?"

"I'm not being paid anything for my testimony. I'm being paid for my time."

"Well, how much will you be paid for your efforts today?"

"That depends in part on how long you intend to keep me here on the stand."

"Well, then, since the taxpayers are paying for all this, I'd better hurry and finish up. Doctor, you said this morning that Mrs. Williams intended only to *change* her husband when she fired that rifle, did you not?"

"Yes."

"Well, she certainly did change him, didn't she?"

"I guess she did."

"No further questions, Doctor."

Despite the prosecutor's effective, no-nonsense cross-examination, the jury found Mrs. Williams not guilty by reason of insanity. The judge sent her to a state hospital for a one-month evaluation so that he might be assured that she was no longer a danger to anyone, including herself. At the hospital she was diagnosed as "a passive-dependent personality, complicated by acute depression, rapidly improving." The hospital recommended that Mrs. Williams receive outpatient treatment—which she did.

Some time thereafter she and her daughter left the state. To the best of my knowledge, she has not come to public attention again.

13
SUMMARY: THE MASOCHISTICALLY DEPENDENT KILLER

EVERYONE IS to some extent dependent upon those he loves, but when one becomes convinced that psychological survival depends *entirely* upon another—only to find that source of sustenance threatened—the stage has been set for some potentially violent behavior. Neither Roland, Julie, Lisa, or Roger could sustain a relationship with their partners—or live without them. On those occasions when one of them might try to let them go, their partners would find ways of clinging to them, long enough to bind them again and reawaken their dependent needs, but never long enough—nor well enough—to meet them. Thus, all four were locked into a state of permanent emotional deprivation, masochistically unable to free themselves to find other resources, yet too fragile to sustain themselves.

My many years of experience with domestic homicides have left me a firm believer in the quick and irrevocable divorce. Couples who try interminably to "work it out," or who endlessly separate and reconcile are asking for trouble. Their unconscious minds know this, even if the rest of them does not.

V

THE PSYCHOPATHIC KILLER

The psychopath at first glance seems quite well-put-together. He suffers neither delusions, hallucinations, nor memory impairment; contact with reality appears solid. Rather, his psychiatric deficit— and it is a substantial one—manifests as a chronic inability to conform behavior to social norms, to defer gratification, control impulses, tolerate frustration, profit from corrective experiences, or identify with others and form meaningful relationships with them.

Nevertheless, the psychopath always knows, cognitively speaking, when he is breaking the law. Though often reckless, he may be constrained by direct surveillance. But not for long. He must have what he wants irrespective of cost to those in his way.

THE THING TO DO

"**T**HEY CAN'T seem to find him, Doctor," said the gate guard at San Quentin Prison, where the examination was scheduled to take place.

I was astonished. "He's on Death Row for having killed three people and you misplace him?"

"This prison's pretty big. We don't have enough staff. But he's around here somewhere," the guard hastened to reassure me. "He's not gonna get far."

It took him an hour to make and receive several phone calls in the service of tracking my man down in the huge and crumbling nineteenth-century penal institution, which glowers at the mainland from a spit of land jutting into the chilled waters of San Francisco Bay.

"Okay, they've got the guy, Dr. Blinder. Should have him in an interview room for you in a few minutes. Take this pass and walk down the brick path to Death Row in Building 20. I'll have to search you first."

By the time we had completed this process, a previously gentle January rain was now driving. Exiting the gatehouse, I reached for my umbrella. "Sorry, Doctor, I'll have to keep that here. No weapons on the prison grounds."

Leaving my dignity with my umbrella, I took off at a fast clip through the sheets of water. I had almost reached the building when a loud whistle blew. A moment later two angry guards grabbed me by the shoulders and forcibly slowed me to a walk, while observing pointedly that a man running across a prison yard runs some risk of being shot. (I saw no profit in discussing with them why they might shoot at someone running *toward* the prison.)

Once inside, my cold, soggy clothes were searched again and my fountain pen examined with some care and only grudgingly returned. I was then led to and locked inside a tiny, windowless room divided into two compartments by a thick Plexiglas wall with an opening the size of a bar of soap. Each compartment had a chair. Nothing more.

After a few minutes, the door to the other compartment was unlocked and opened. A classically handsome man of about thirty was released from handcuffs and ankle shackles; he entered and settled easily into the mean metal chair as if he was the head of the house returning to his accustomed Lazy Boy Recliner. He flashed me a smile the luminosity of which far exceeded that of the naked lightbulb hanging above our heads, reached through the hole in the partition for my hand, and greeted me in an anchorman's voice.

"Hi, I'm Ken. My attorney told me you were coming. You look kinda wet."

"I *am* kinda wet."

"Isn't California weather awful? I'm sure sorry I ever came here."

I shook his hand and we exchanged criticisms of our facilities. Then I asked if he understood why his appeals attorney had asked me to see him.

"I think so. He said that it was a glaring oversight for me not to have pled insane or something of the sort at the time of my trial. He said that even though I'd been convicted, we could bring up any new evidence or arguments at any time. Right up to the moment I get snuffed."

"That's about right. Let me ask you—what do *you* think? Do you think there was something wrong with your head when you killed those people?"

"*I* didn't kill those people. Karen did . . ."

"I know that's what you said in your trial . . ."

"That's what I said in my trial, that's what I told the police, that's what I told my attorney, that's what I told the guy handling the appeal, and that's what I'm telling you."

"That your girlfriend Karen killed them."

"Right."

"But she turned state's evidence and testified that you had killed them . . ."

"Yeah . . ."

"And the jury believed her."

"Well, I guess so, 'cause here I sit here and she doesn't."

"I must tell you, Ken, I've reviewed all the evidence and read the trial transcript twice. I also believe Karen. What she said has the ring of truth. What you said does not."

"Yeah, well, it doesn't really matter now what you believe, does it, Doctor?"

"Probably not. But consider this: Your attorney is preparing an appeal—though I gather there really are no grounds for one, save the possible issue of your state of mind at the time of your offense; it's not every day that someone gratuitously kills three people. Admittedly, from everything I've read, offhand I don't really see where mental illness is an issue in this case. But it's worth exploring, and I'm here to explore it with you—if only because nothing else but a technicality stands between you and the gas chamber."

"They execute innocent people all the time . . ."

"And you have a right to maintain that innocence up to the very end. Whether anyone believes you or not. Thus far, apparently nobody does. That includes your lawyers. As you know, they do not think you have anything to lose, but possibly—possibly—something to gain if you can be candid with me. And candid you must be. Obviously I cannot determine your state of mind at the time of a crime you did not commit."

"But right now you don't see a mental case here?"

"Frankly, at this point, I don't. I can't give you a definite answer on that, though, without examining what it was that was going on in your head when those people were killed. If you simply didn't do it, fine. Like I said, you need not persuade me of anything. But if there *is* something about your mental state that the court should know, if I examine you I will most certainly find it and make the appropriate report to your attorney. If I find nothing, he'll hear about that too. It's your choice. I have the entire afternoon available for you if you want it. Or we can call it a day."

Ken lit a cigarette and smoked and thought. He finished it, put it out, and lit another.

"All right, I'll tell you what happened."

Ken's story began some three years before when, while tending bar in Bullhead, South Dakota, he poured a Mrs. Karen Dwight and her girlfriend Bloody Marys and within moments fell in love.

"At first, I didn't know what had happened to me. I couldn't take my eyes off of her. Like . . . everybody else in the bar disappeared all of a sudden and she and I were alone. I don't think I said more than three words to her —hell, I could hardly catch my breath. I've never experienced anything like that before."

It was true. Ken had managed to get through almost three decades without connecting in an emotional way with anyone. Certainly not with his parents, whom he described as correct, but cold. They conceived him because they decided they ought to have a child, then afterward thought better of it and left him in the care of a series of housekeepers. He slid through high school, floated in and out of a local college, was drafted and shortly thereafter dishonorably discharged for repeatedly being absent without leave. He then drifted from state to state, undertaking odd jobs and an occasional, careless, petty theft. At the time he met Karen he had been in jail perhaps a dozen times, though never for more than a month for any conviction. His social life had been equally indifferent: never a close friend, female or male, but many casual lovers of both sexes. With men he usually exchanged sex for money.

"It was really all the same to me. I had sex a lot, but I could take it or leave it. Then I met Karen and I wanted it all the time, I wanted her all the time, I only wanted to be with her."

Karen came back to the bar the next night, this time without her girlfriend, and this time she and Ken talked. When the bar closed, they went to his room.

"I didn't know sex could be like that. I would lose myself inside her. No—I didn't even have to be inside her—just a few kisses and I could no longer think, I could only feel. I would almost drown in the fragrance of her hair, her breath, the crack between her breasts, her pussy —they all smelled different, they all smelled wonderful. I'd take a few sniffs and get high. And the way she fucked me, went down on me, even just touched me—she'd take me apart. The more she gave me, the more I wanted. I could never get enough. She told me I was the best lover she'd ever had. Christ! *I* didn't do anything. I just went for it."

Karen's husband, a rancher of some sort, made it difficult, though not impossible, for his wife to be out of the house overnight; but daytime liasons were much easier, so she and Ken agreed to meet the next afternoon for lunch. Early that morning, Ken went to the bar, cleaned the previous night's take out of the till, and met Karen for lunch. Lunch consisted of about a third of a Bloody Mary for each and then they were back in his room. Karen was supposed to be home by six o'clock. They didn't look at a watch until well past eight. Karen hurried out, still buttoning her blouse, just minutes before a police officer arrived and arrested Ken for stealing two hundred and forty dollars from his employer's bar.

Though consisting largely of trivia, the length of Ken's rap sheet coupled with the relative novelty of crime in the tiny town convinced the circuit judge to deliver Ken to the three-cell county jail for six months. Karen visited him every day.

One afternoon, toward the end of the first month of Ken's sentence, he called the jailer, complaining of an upset stomach, and asked for some Alka-Seltzer. The jailer complied. A few minutes later Ken shouted that he had thrown up—could he have the mop and bucket? The jailer brought Ken what he wanted, opened the cell door, and handed the equipment to him. Ken grabbed the mop and smashed the handle on the jailer's head, took his gun, and raced out the back door, where Karen was waiting in her husband's Lincoln. They headed west.

"We didn't cover a lot of ground. We would drive for an hour and then get so hot we'd pull over and fuck in the back seat. Or we'd stop overnight in a motel and stay in bed until noon. Karen was delicious. Completely edible. No pits, seeds, or tough skin. Neither of us could get enough of the other. It took us an entire week just to get to Denver."

"And you were never stopped by the police looking for you or Karen's car?"

"Not once. The entire trip."

By the time they arrived in Grand Junction they were about out of money. Karen's husband did not believe in credit cards, and while Karen had some jewelry, there was no practical way she could sell it for a fraction of its value. So they decided to trade the spare Michelin in the

Lincoln's trunk at a gas station for some gas and extra cash.

Unfortunately, it was the time of the great gasoline crisis and the station attendant was not inclined to deal. "This ain't no fuckin' trading post," he had told Ken, and turned back into the office.

Ken took the jailer's stolen revolver, followed and caught up with the attendant in the office, held the gun to his head, and made him empty out the cash register. Then he pulled the trigger.

"Why, for heaven's sake?"

"I don't know. It just seemed like the thing to do. I hadn't intended to kill him. I'd never really hurt anyone before. But Karen was waiting in the car. I wanted to get back to her and it was the quickest way to handle things."

"Karen must have heard the shot . . ."

"She didn't say a word. She just drank up the beer we had in the car and sang to me all the way to Vegas. There she was hotter than ever. We screwed around and gambled, won some money, got a lot of free booze, lost our winnings, and screwed around some more. I think it was the happiest time of my life.

"We hung out there about four days and then started toward California. We didn't get very far, though, when something happened to the car. It wouldn't go more than about twenty-five miles an hour. We got as far as a trailer park and spent the night there. In the morning, some woman was leaving and we told her about our car problem and got her to take us toward town. As soon as we came to a quiet stretch in the road, I pulled out the gun and made her stop and get out. I shot her in the head, took her wallet, and dragged her into a deep culvert alongside the road. Then we turned her car around and headed toward Los Angeles."

"What did you feel when you shot her?"

"Nothing. I didn't feel anything. It was simply an easy, obvious solution to a small problem."

"And Karen . . ."

"Like it never happened. Nothing was happening, nothing mattered except our touching each other."

Ken and Karen continued to drive west, on the way passing a young female hitchhiker with knapsack and guitar. Ken slowed the car down to pick her up. "What's the point?" Karen had asked and Ken assured her that he recognized the type: a pseudo-hippy with hobo pretensions and lots of Daddy's money. Karen reminded him that he couldn't simply rob her and let it go at that. "I know," he had replied.

The hitchhiker was quite cordial and the three of them got along well. Karen sang to their passenger's guitar accompaniment. After a while Ken announced that he needed a pit stop. The ladies could join him if they didn't mind using the bushes. They all agreed. Once out of sight of the road, Ken again drew his revolver and shot the young woman in the head.

"Any fear, any remorse, any thoughts or feelings?"

"Not that I can recall, Doctor."

"I suppose you robbed her as well."

"Yes. I was wrong about her, though. She had all of twelve dollars." He smiled his brilliant smile. "I've never been a good judge of people."

That night Ken and Karen reached Los Angeles, found a quiet, cheap motel, and lived there for four months, off the sale of Karen's jewelry. During most of that time, their passion ran unabated. Save for meals and occasional purchases, they rarely left their room. The last few weeks, however, Karen's ardor cooled a bit. One day she went out, ostensibly to pick up fresh cosmetics, but did not return. Instead the police came and Ken immediately gave himself up. Shortly thereafter he was tried for murder. Karen was given immunity and testified for the prosecution. After listening to her for a day, the jury convicted Ken and sentenced him to death.

15
SUMMARY:
THE PSYCHOPATHIC KILLER

THOUGH CERTAINLY capable of lust and anger, the psychopathic killer is the media's "cold-blooded murderer." He kills not because of stress or disability, but for profit. Twenty dollars will do. Unable to identify or empathize with others and insensitive to all but his own immediate passions, he sees the lives of his victims as having little consequence. He kills casually, without remorse.

Clearly, psychopaths (in current psychiatric parlance, called *sociopaths* because they possess an "antisocial character disorder") have a piece missing. This mental defect, originating early in childhood, separates them from the rest of humanity and results in a lack of empathy for it. Yet they are otherwise rational, logical, appropriate, competent, even charming and persuasive. While some are so disordered and out-of-control that they spend entire lives behind bars for one offense after another, others, whose sociopathy is either partial or relatively subtle, can be quite successful in life. Unfettered by conscience or the sensibilities of others, they may quickly amass fortunes, power, and a following of admirers until slowed and finally dragged to a halt by the weight of broken rules and broken hearts everywhere around them.

Ken, a classical psychopath, had but two goals—having Karen and getting to California. The concerns, pain, or survival of anyone who might inconvenience him were of no import. Karen reciprocated Ken's singular lust—which may have been in tune with a large sociopathic streak of her own—although, in time, even she came to experience fear and remorse no longer repressible by sex, however incendiary. Still, during the height of her passion she provided a catalyst that potentiated her lover's sociopathy, enabling him to evolve effortlessly from misdemeanant to multimurderer.

Ken's eventual candor with me permitted a diagnosis of his character disorder and some understanding of his offenses, but certainly no legal "excuse." Ken had anticipated that. As I gathered my papers together and prepared to leave the interview, he too rose, knocked on the door on his side of the interview room to alert the guard that we were done, and asked:

"Well, Doctor Blinder, I don't suppose you can help me, can you?"

I shook my head.

"Yeah—I didn't think so." He grinned. "What the fuck."

AFTERWORD
THE KILLER AND
THE INSANITY DEFENSE

T HE MENTAL PROCESSES that impel men and women to kill, crisply delineated on paper, blur and overlap in the killers themselves. The ordinarily competent individual who suddenly finds himself ensnared in an emotionally debilitating trap has much in common with those who are both constitutionally powerless and masochistically dependent, and all three act in a way so contrary to their usual conduct as to suggest a dissociative reaction. The disorganized psychotic and the clear-thinking psychopath, though at opposite ends of the diagnostic spectrum, are both psychologically incomplete; and both kill for highly personal, insular, intrapsychic reasons to which their victims make little contribution.

Nevertheless, in each of the several hundred killers I have examined during two decades of court work, a clinical pattern connotive of one of the five diagnostic groups delineated here clearly predominated; and while each individual colored these common pathways with his own unique complexion, we find certain themes—powerlessness, dissociation with suppression of anger, masochistic dependency, psychosis, and sociopathy—recurring again and again. Would that we could identify and help people harboring these processes before their illumination by murder.

While Ken repeatedly chose to kill, the others had far less control over doing what they did. Excluding Ken, the killers you have met in these pages were not so much "criminals" (in the sense of being antisocial citizens who congenitally hold all mores and laws in contempt) as they were simply anguished souls or even ordinary people temporarily overwhelmed by circumstances and their own psychological disabilities.

Unlike true criminals, such killers make little effort to control their offenses—invariably committed at a time when their minds are beyond such precautions, and in a fashion ensuring their detection and capture. Subsequently they talk freely to arresting officers and almost always make full confessions. Their only remaining shield—and it is an appropriate one—is a plea of insanity.

By contrast, the true criminal favors stealth, denial, alibis, and his right to remain silent. He eschews the insanity defense as no defense at all because it requires as a first prerequisite an admission of guilt. In short, the insanity defense is neither intended for nor desired by the inveterate offender. It exists so that the law can distinguish those whose criminality warrants its most crushing vengeance from those whose relative psychological innocence mandates that society's interest be best served by their diversion into a mental health system.

Admittedly, the severity of the defendant's illness does not always correlate well with trial outcome—verdict or sentence; judges, attorneys, and jurors, like psychiatrists, are inconsistent and imperfect, i.e., human. Furthermore, though few defendants actually employ the insanity defense (and very few of those who do will prevail), the attention given a few dramatic insanity trials with psychologically and legally appropriate—but socially and politically unpalatable—outcomes does indeed create the appearance of a widely used or abused process.* Nevertheless, I believe the insanity defense worth preserving, so long as we wish to acknowledge different degrees of culpability and thus, the appropriateness of different degrees and forms of punishment. Even in the flat, monochromatic world of law, if black is to have meaning, there must also be shades of gray.

* For example, in Wyoming, between March of 1975 and February of 1977, 12,307 persons were charged with felonies or crimes punishable by more than one year in prison. At the end of that two-year period, University of Wyoming students surveyed by psychological pollsters regarding their perception of the use of the insanity defense in their state, estimated that one-third of these felons had pleaded not guilty by reason of insanity, and of these, about half had been so adjudicated. In point of fact only 104 (0.8%) defendants utilized the plea, and of these, only four (4%) were found not guilty by reason of insanity. Estimates made by local community residents were as far off the mark as those of the students. ("Altering Opinions About the Insanity Defense," by Richard W. Jeffrey, M.A., and Richard A. Pasewark, Ph.D., *The Journal of Psychiatry and Law,* Spring 1983.)